Simone Sereni

In the Land of Wonders

Coloring Pages with Extraordinary Animal Portraits

Coloring Book

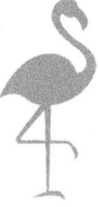

ISBN: 9798863076768

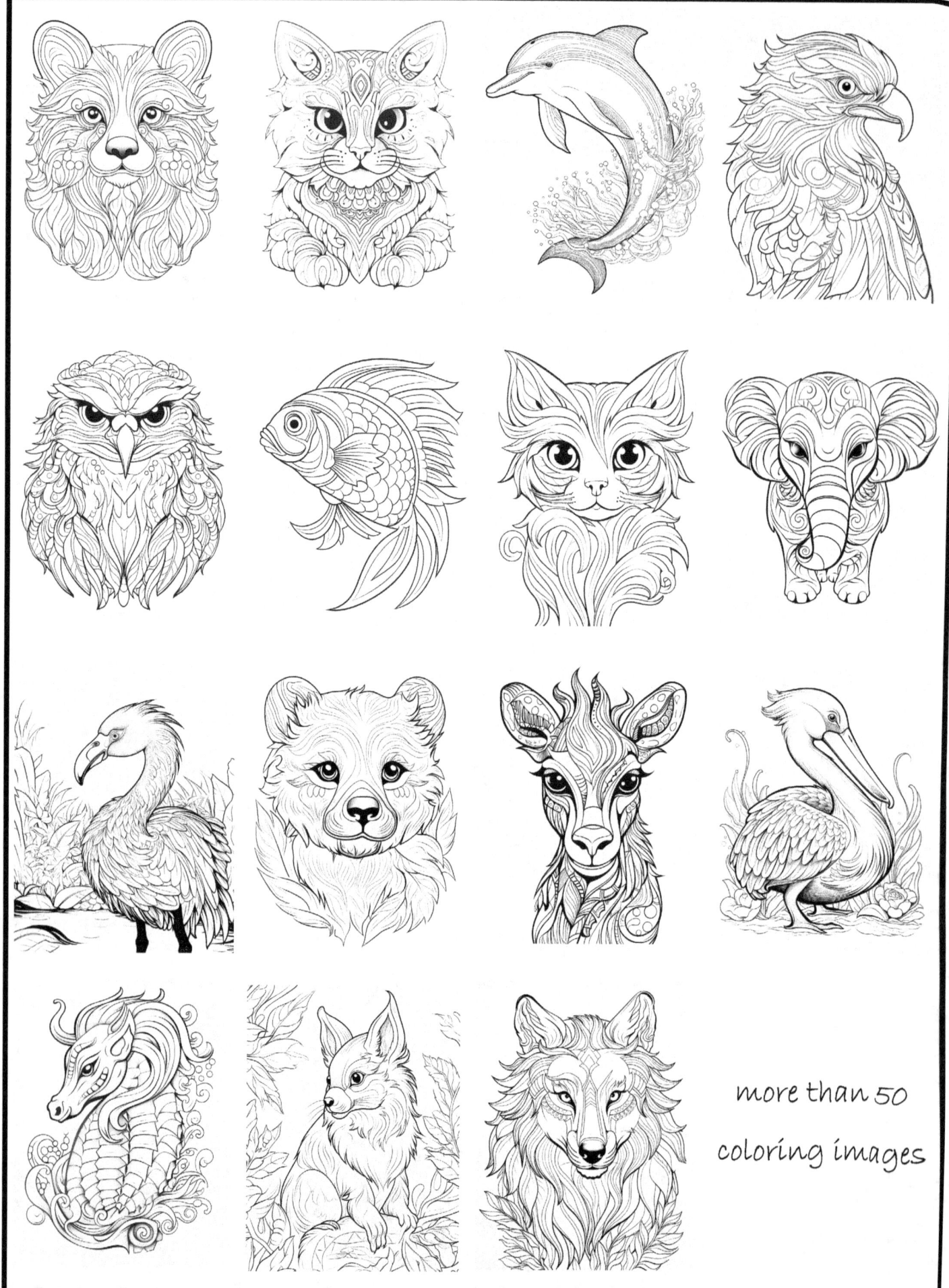

more than 50 coloring images

Color Test Page

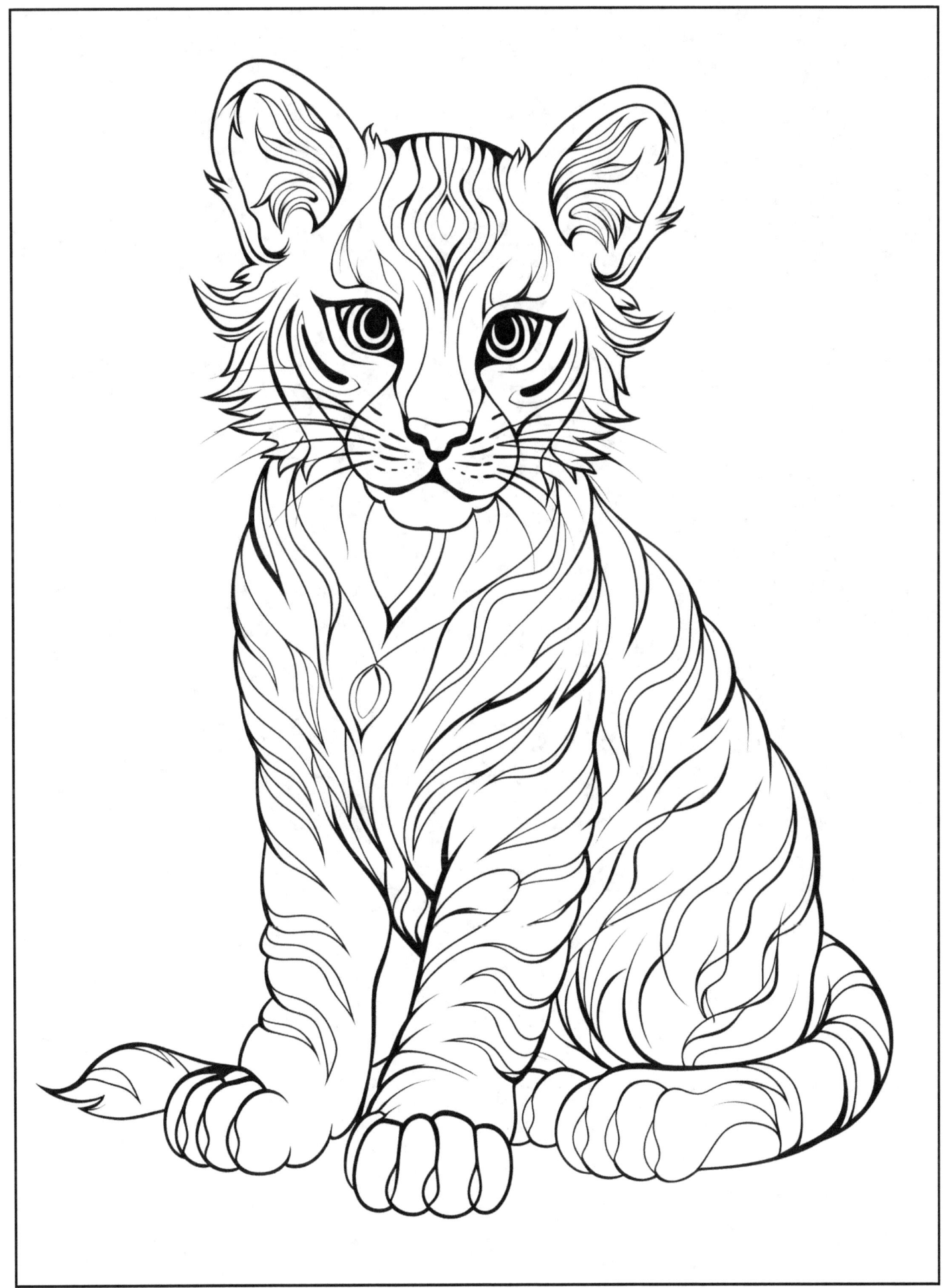

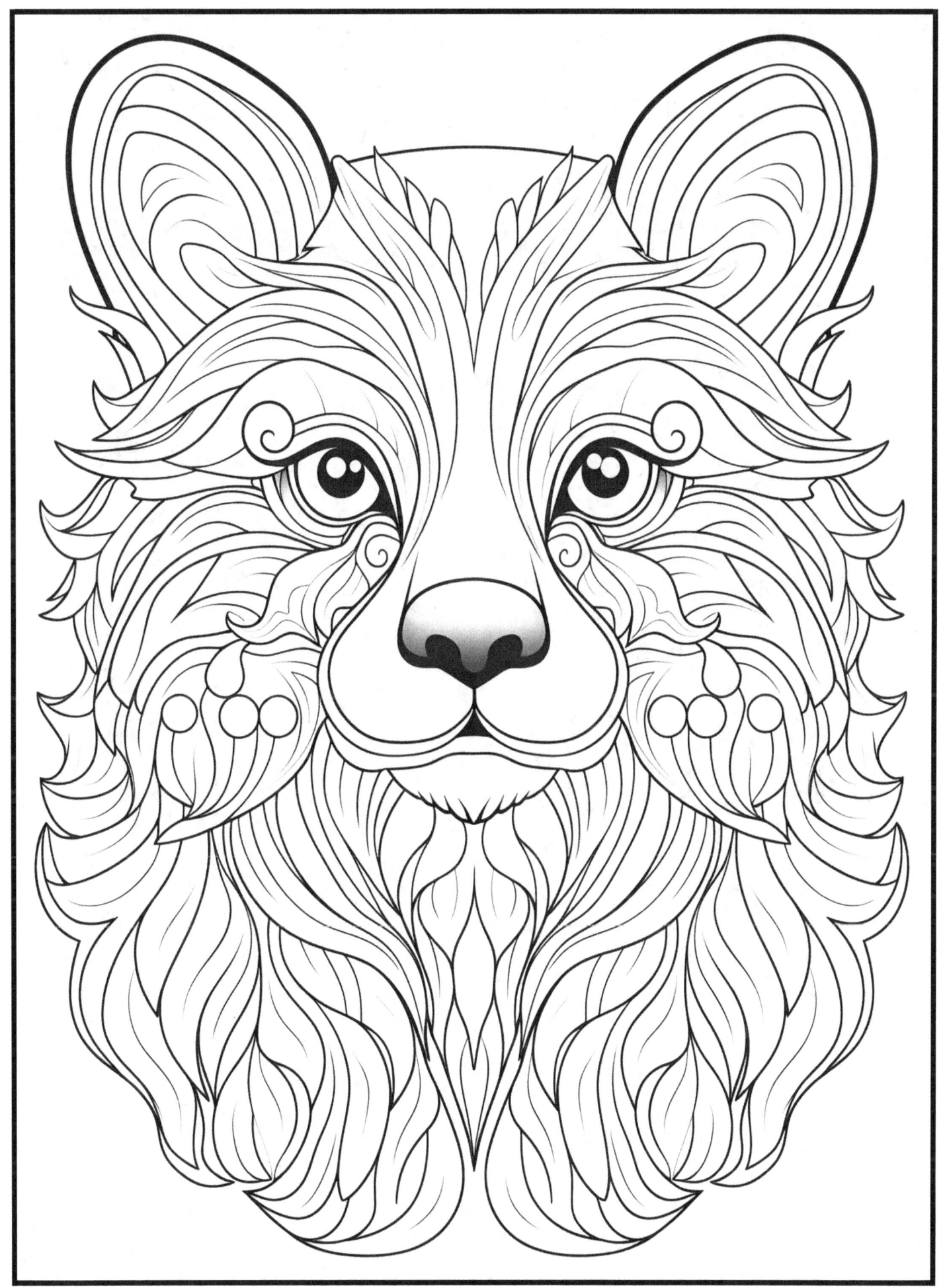

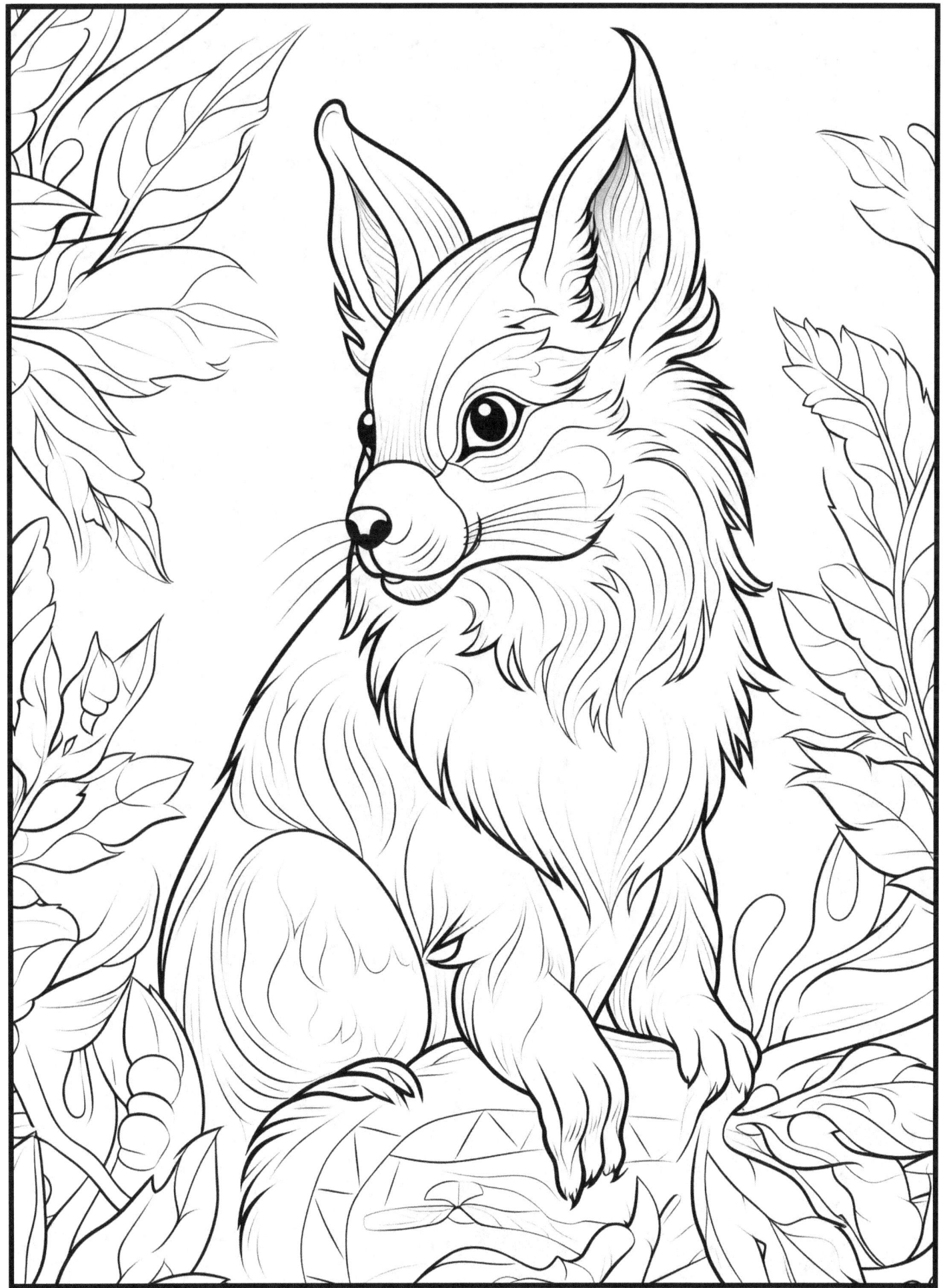

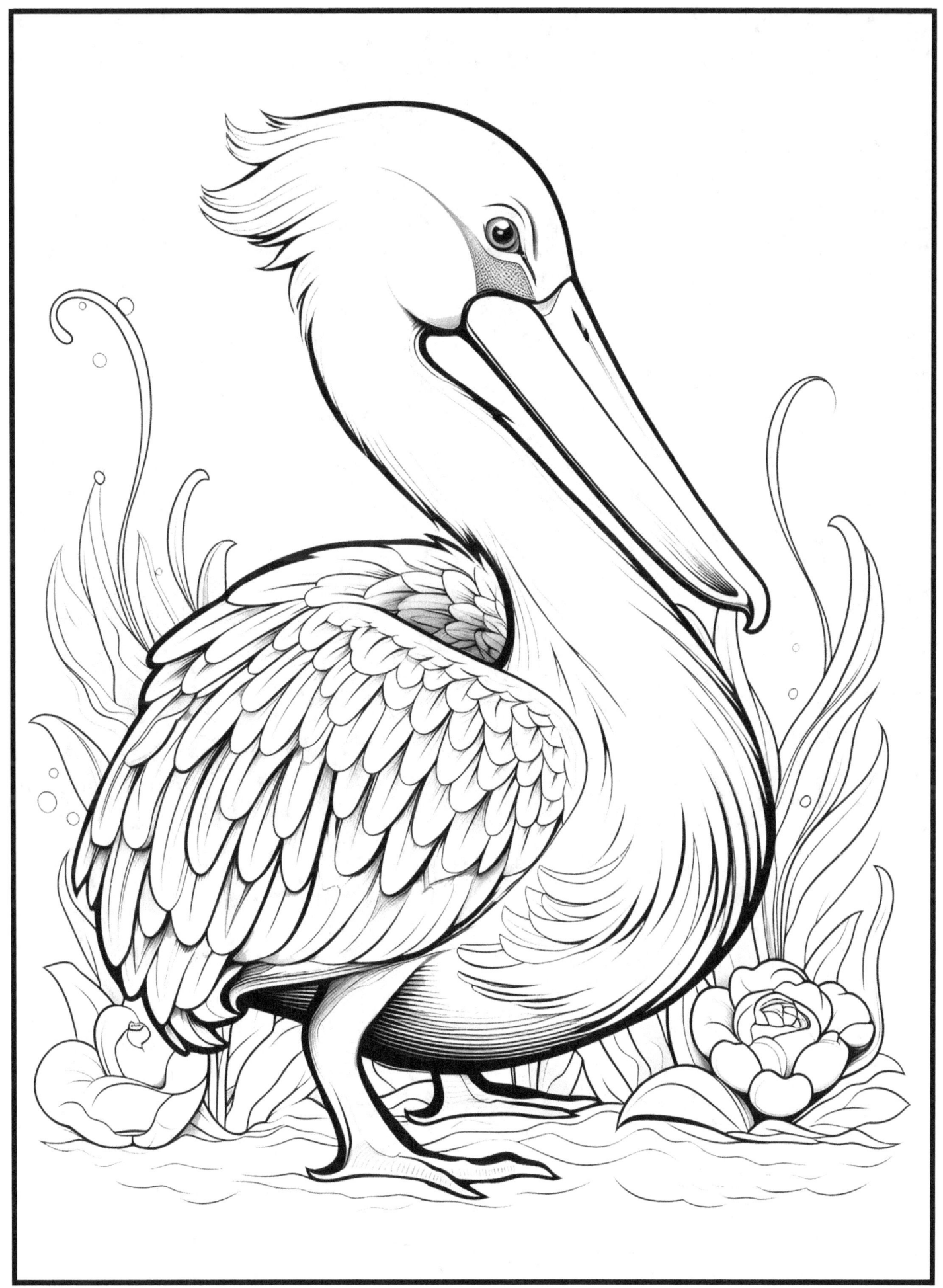

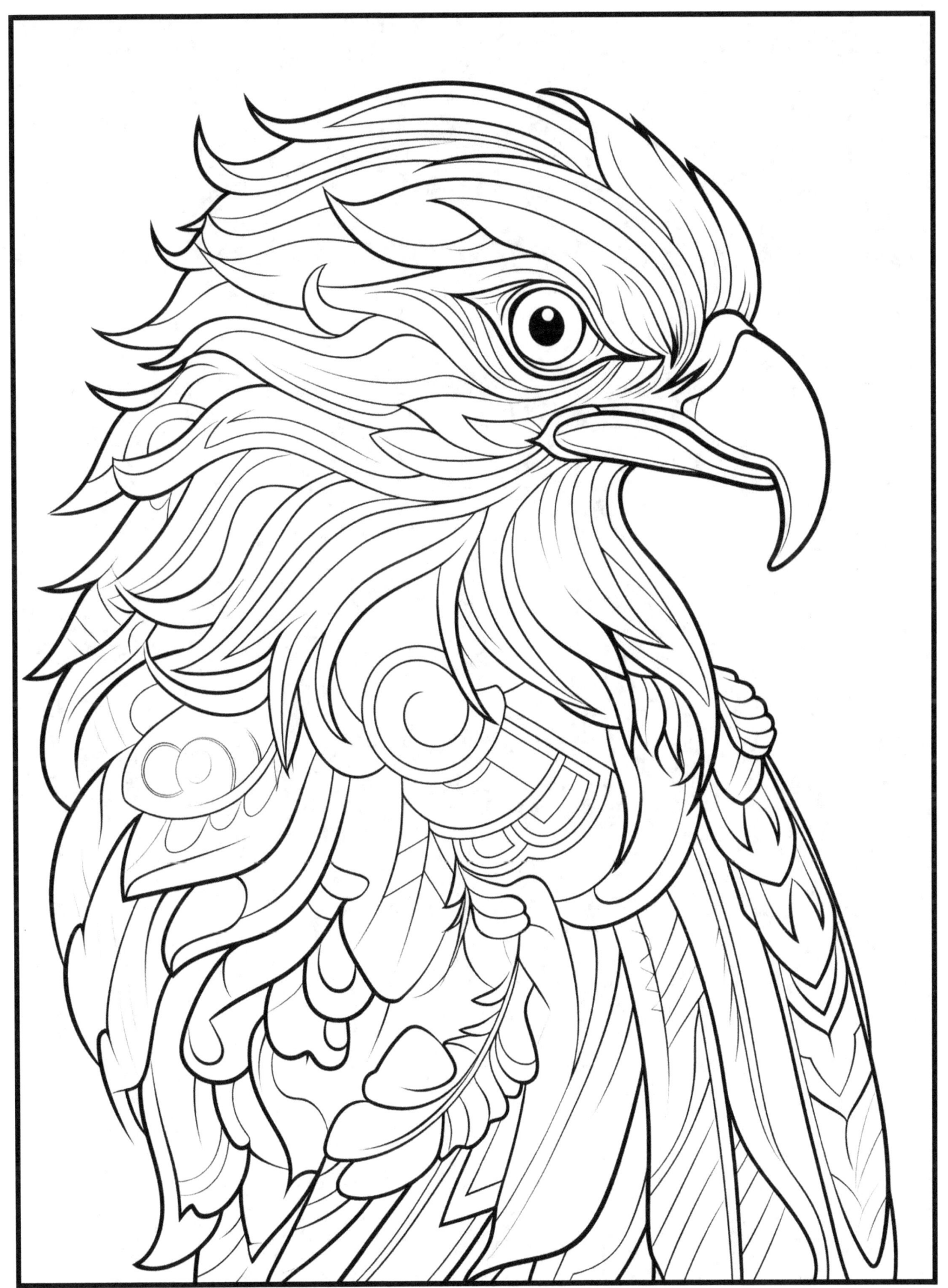

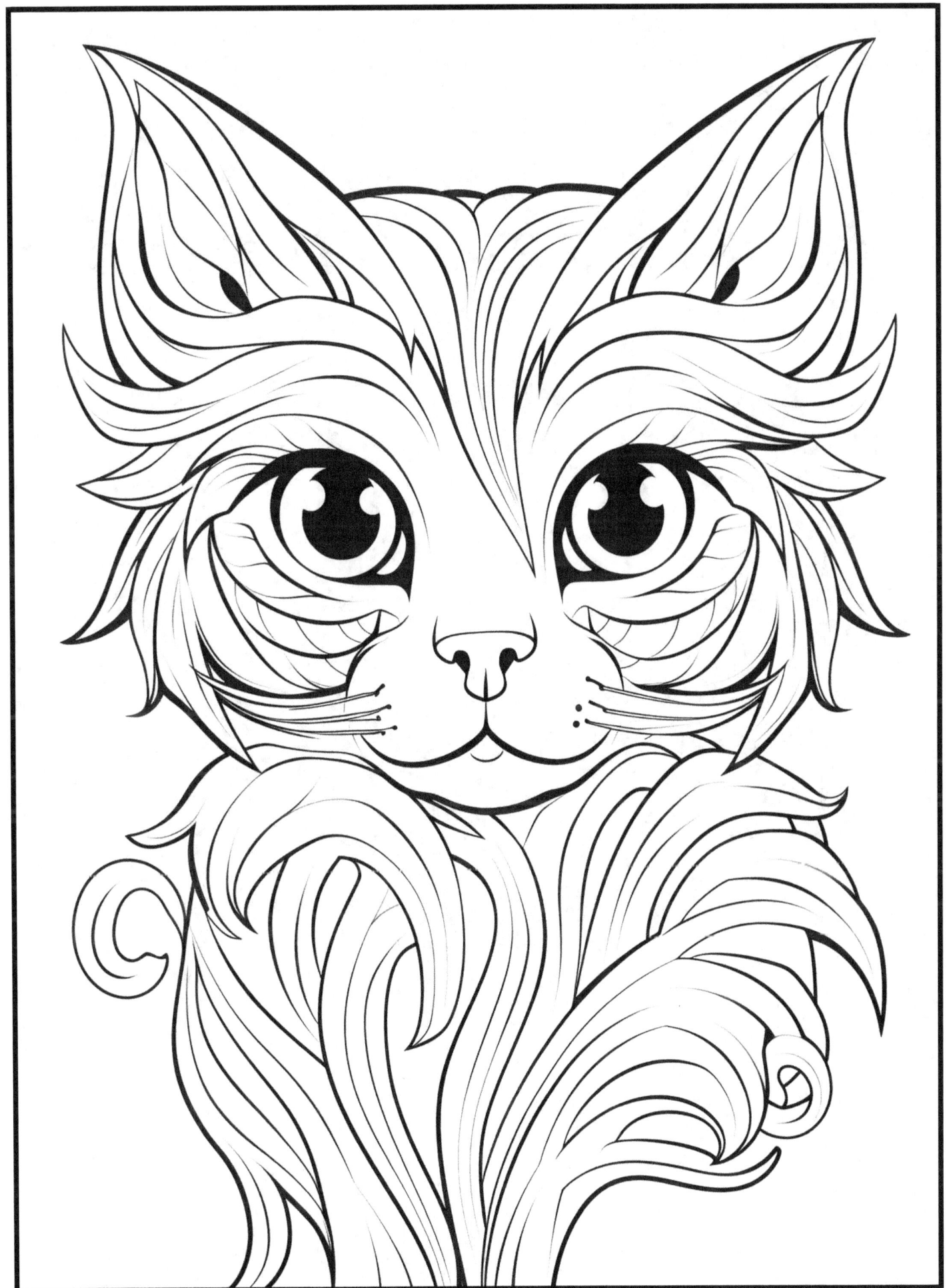

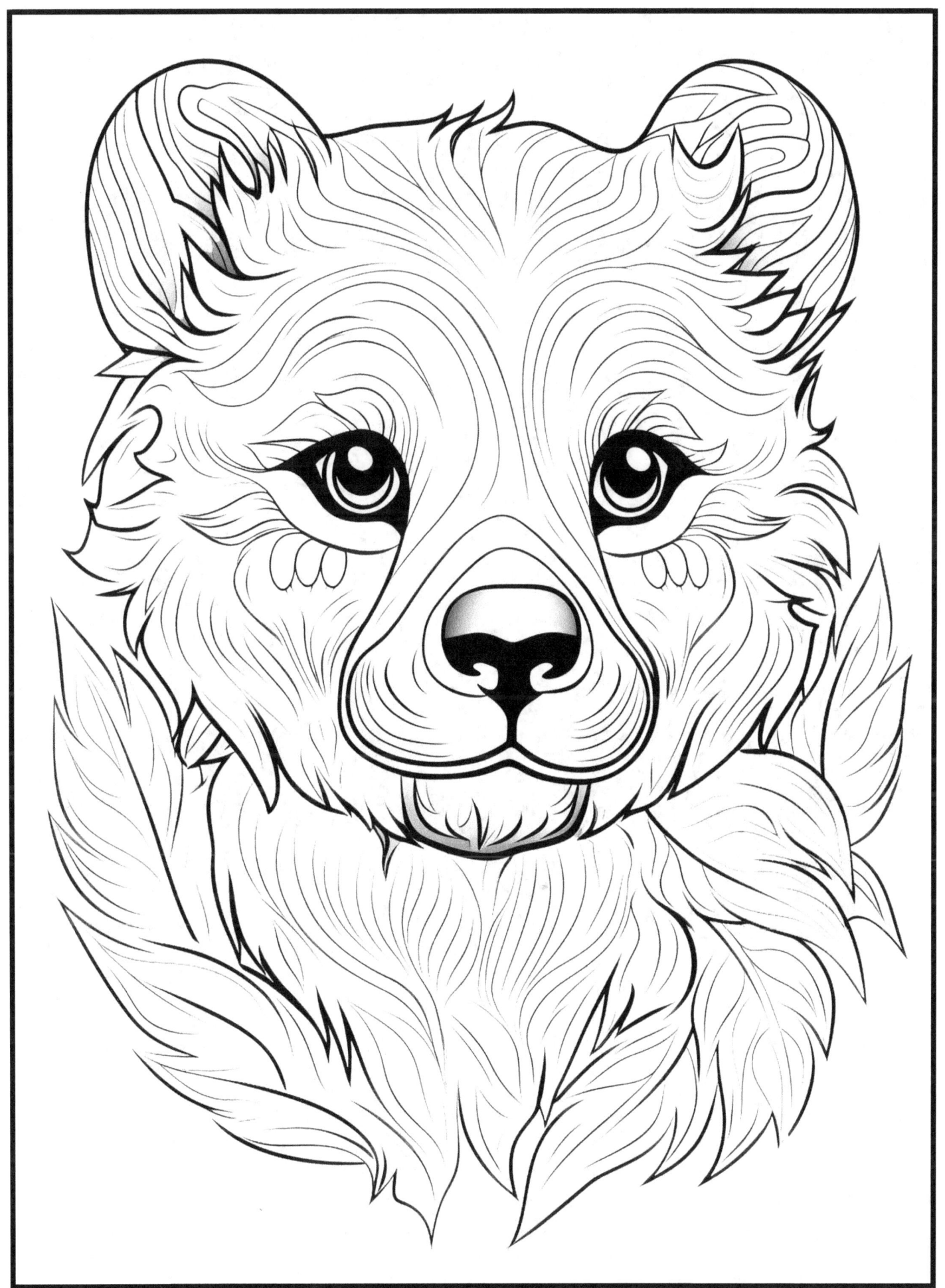

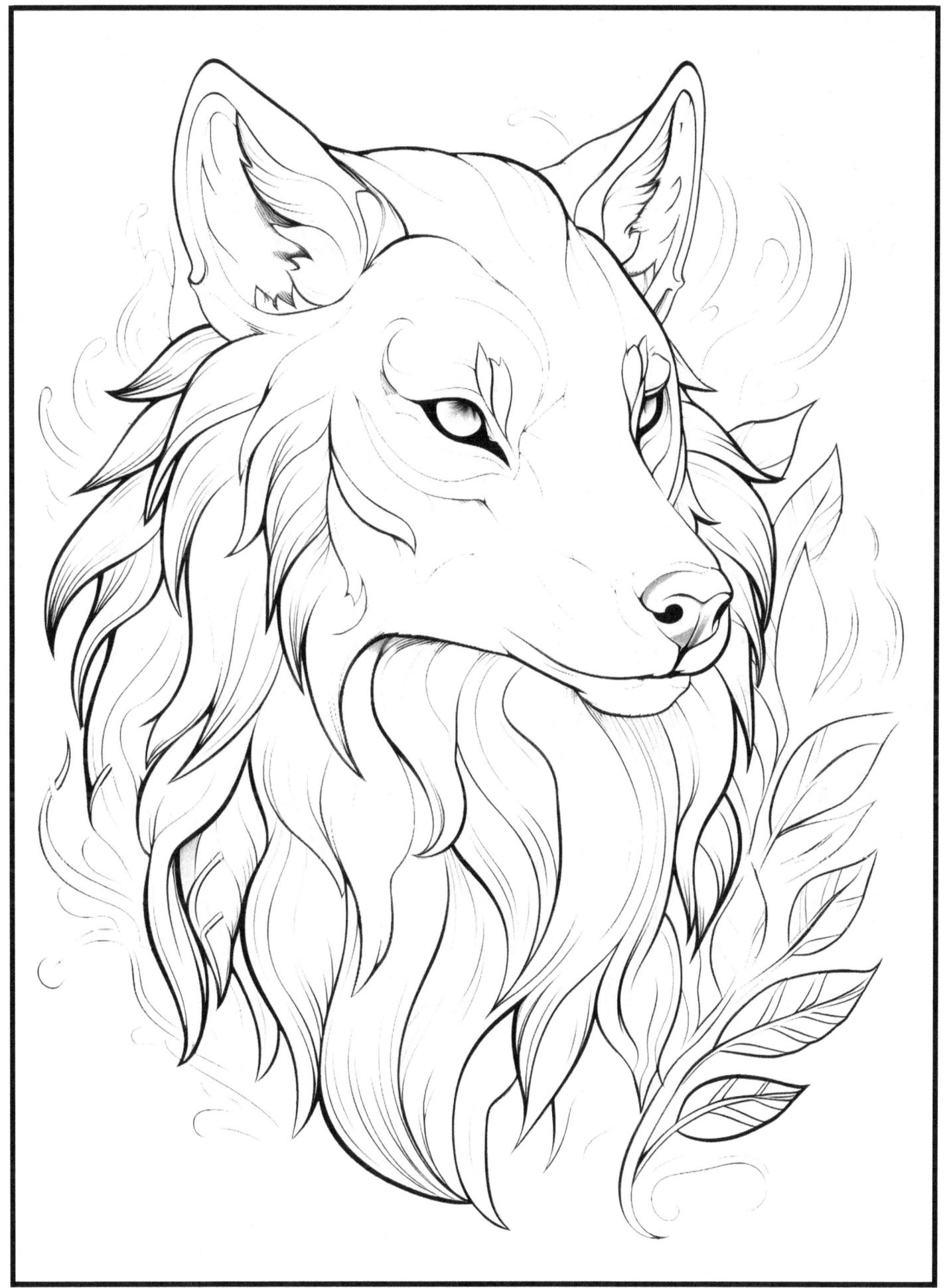

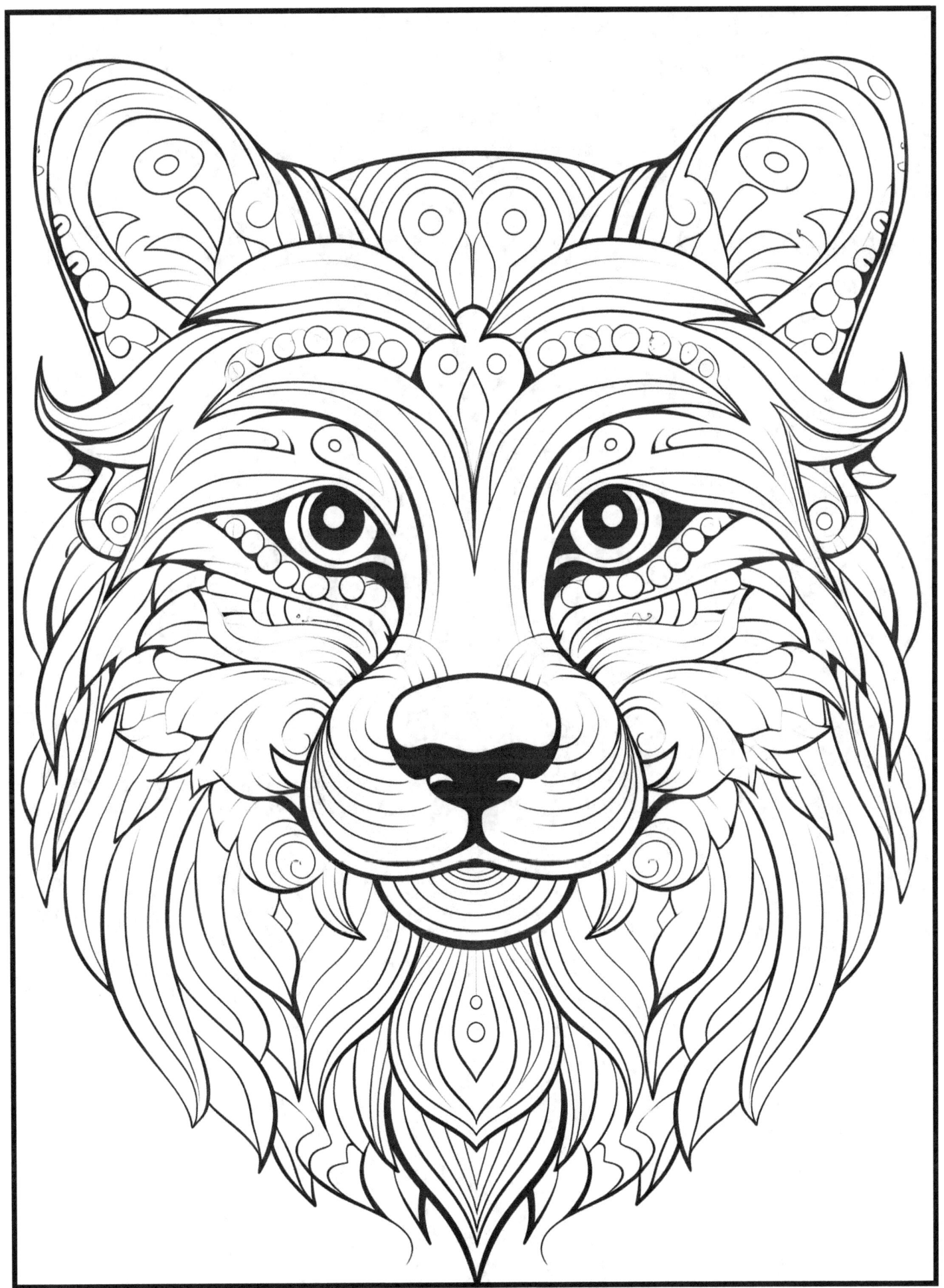

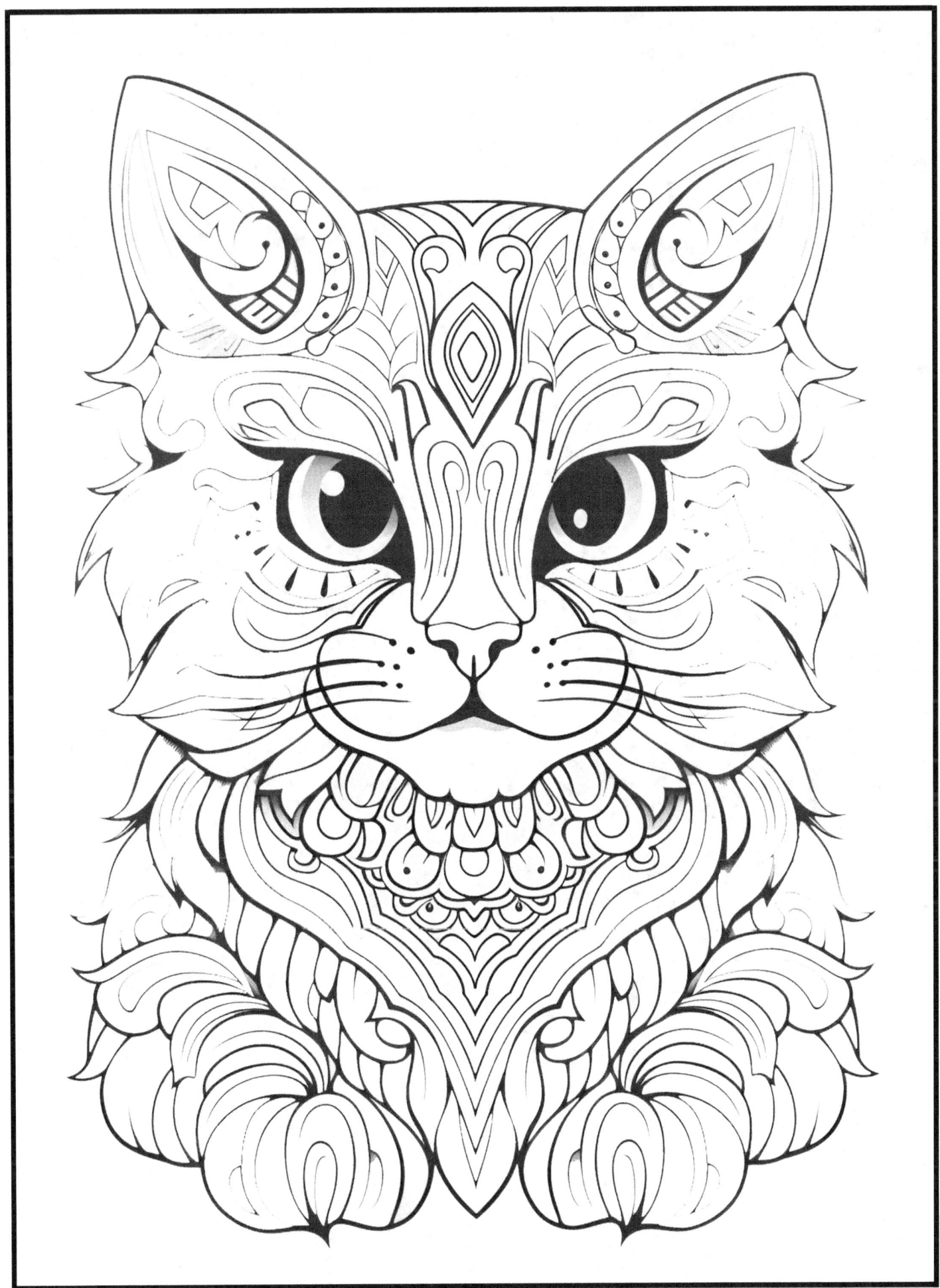

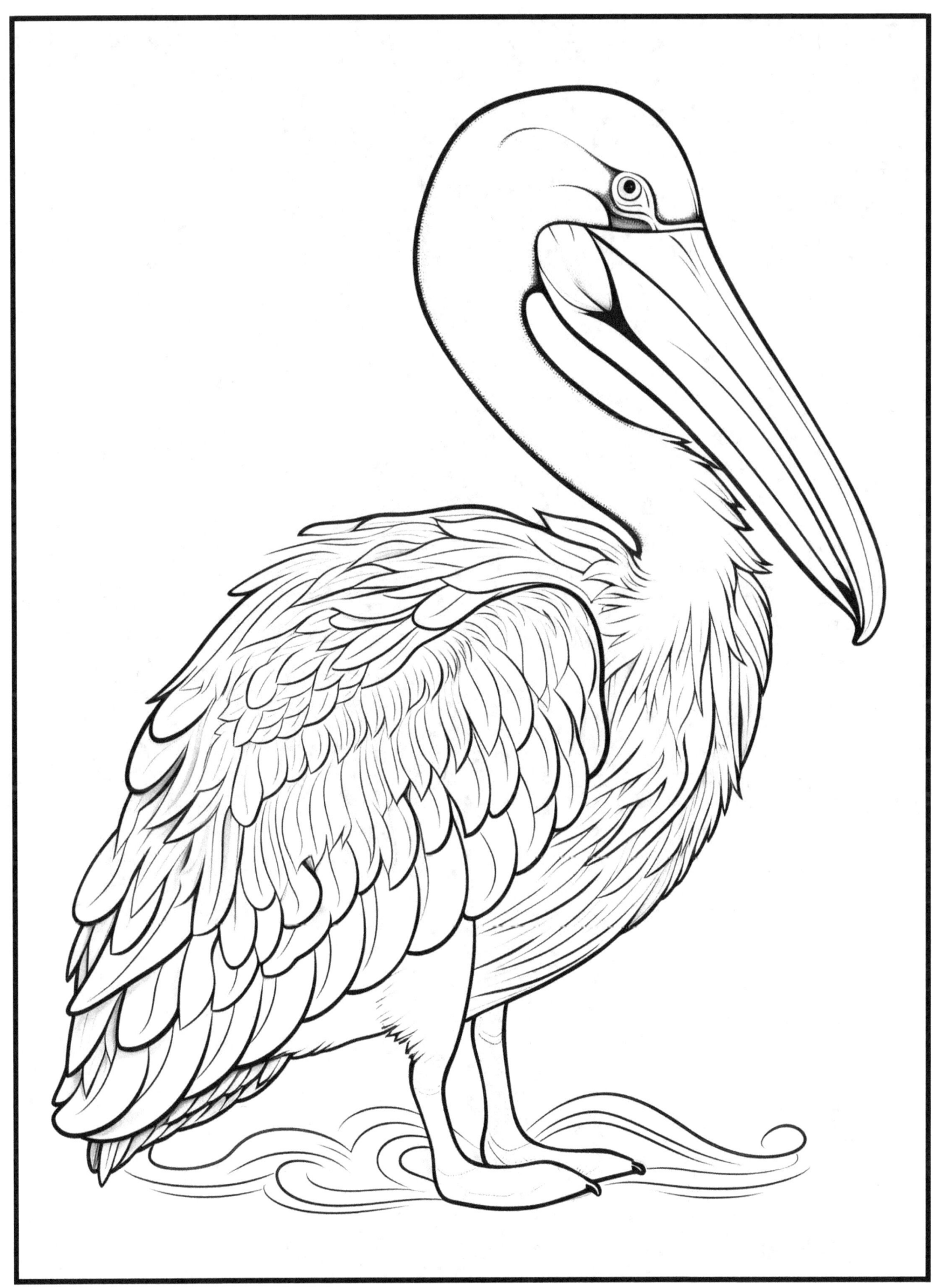

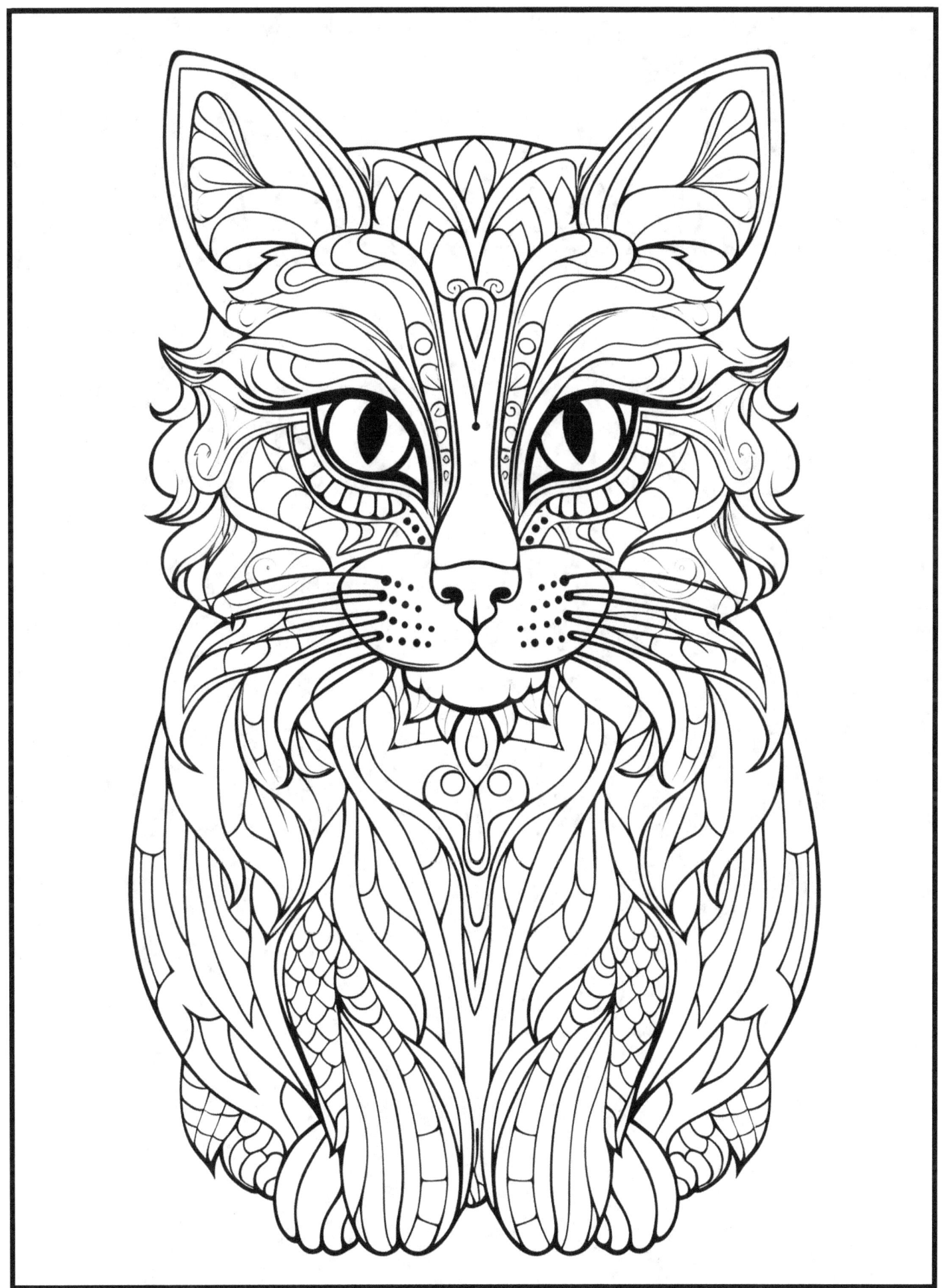

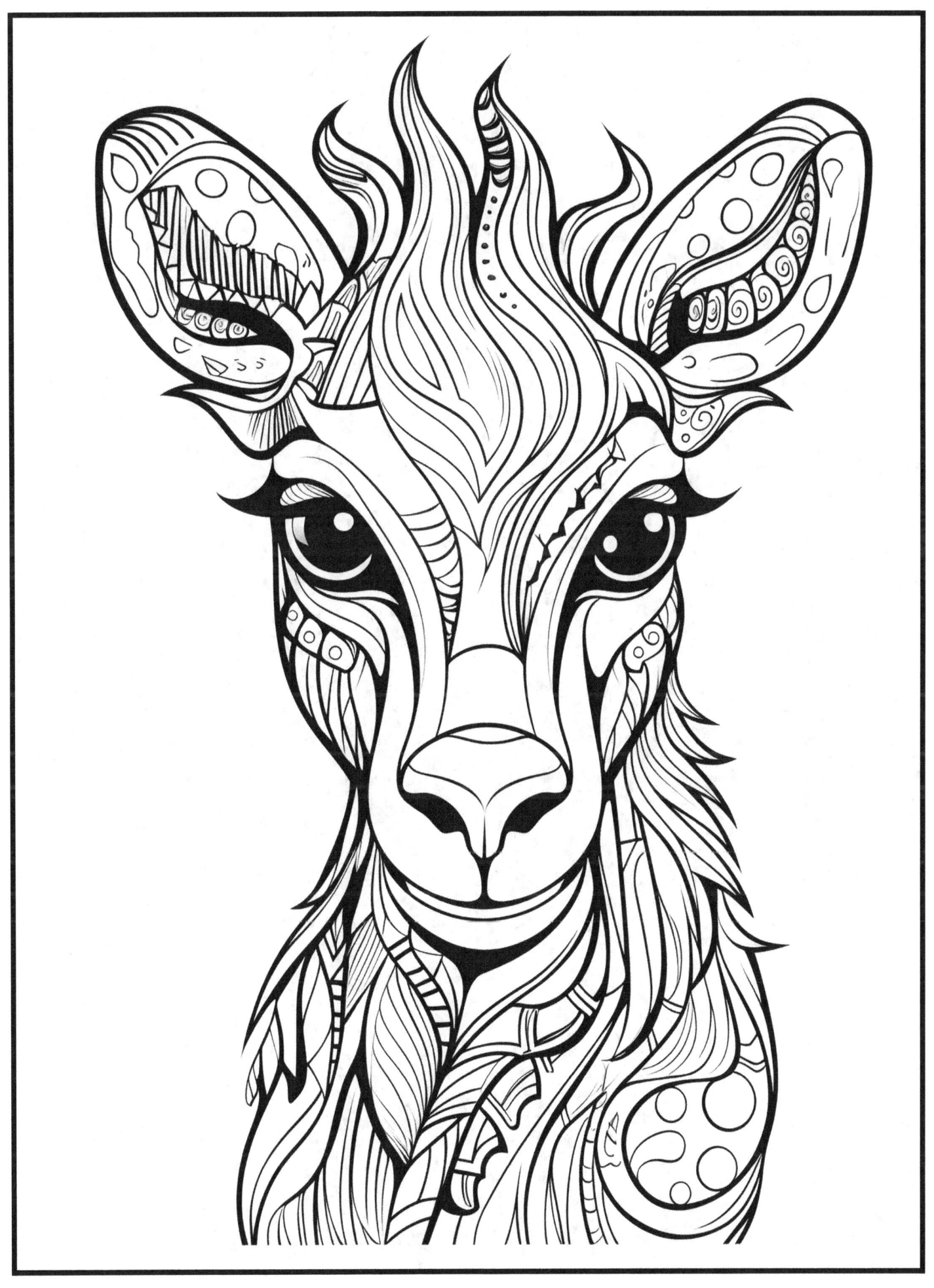

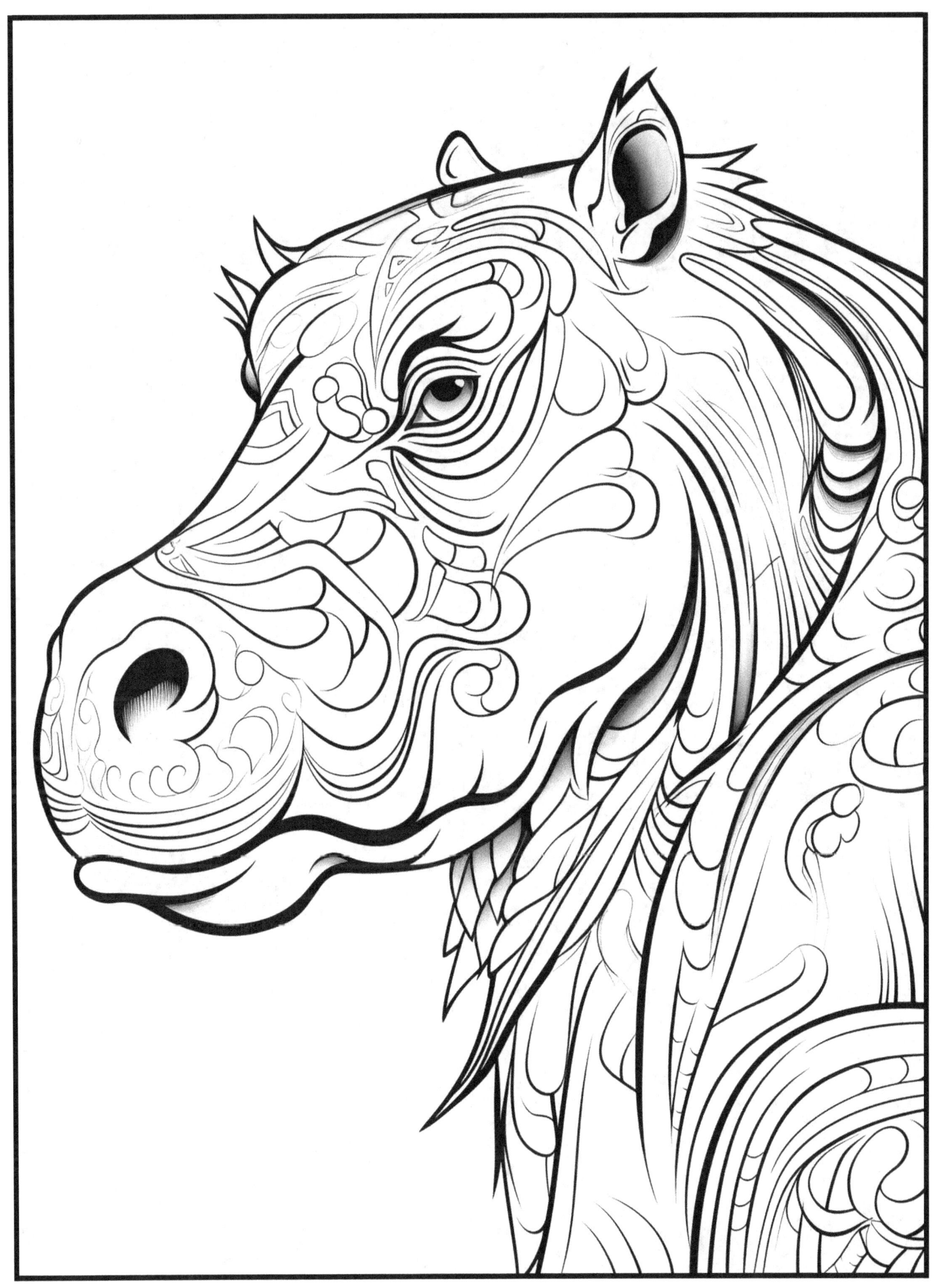

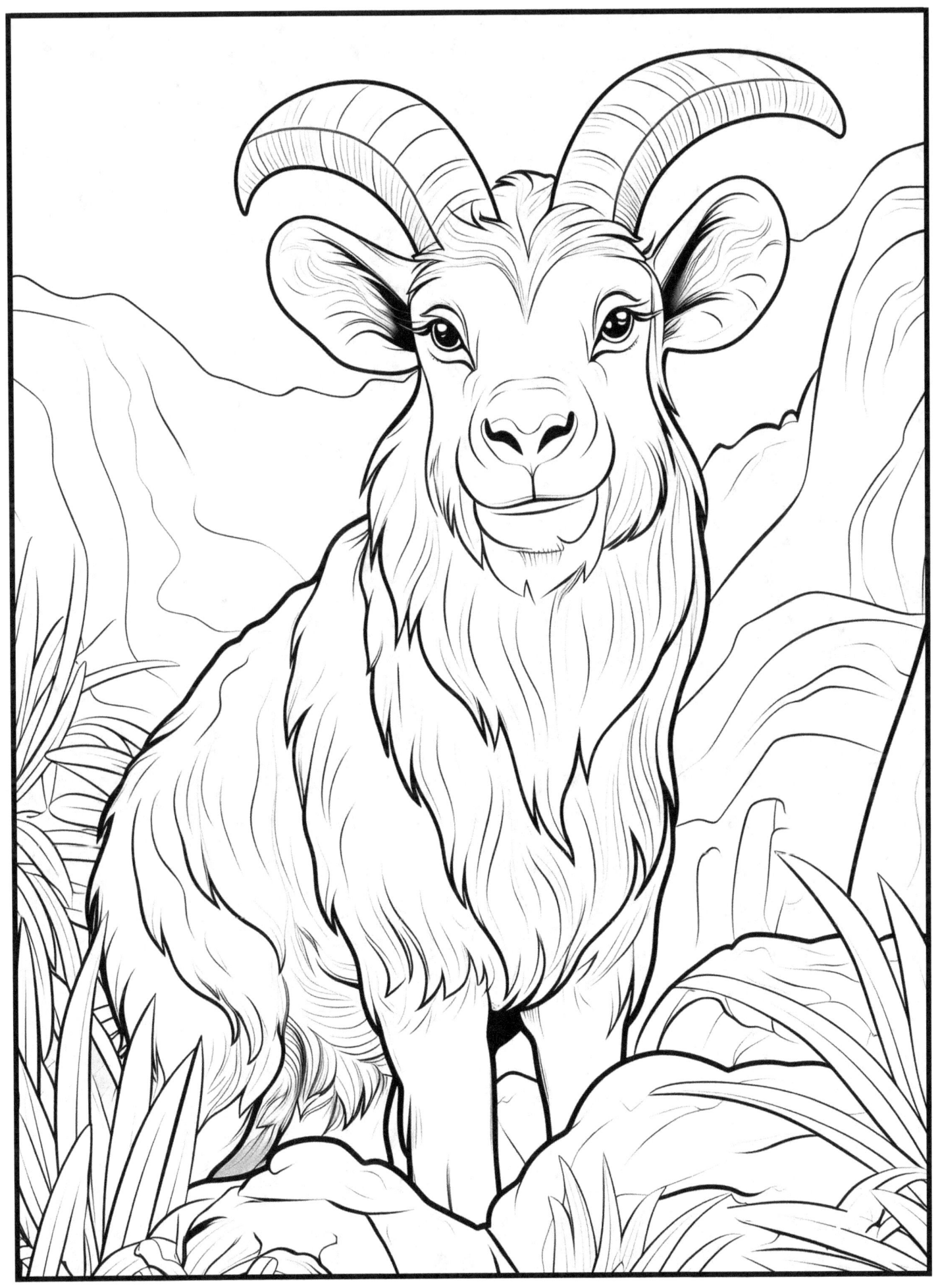

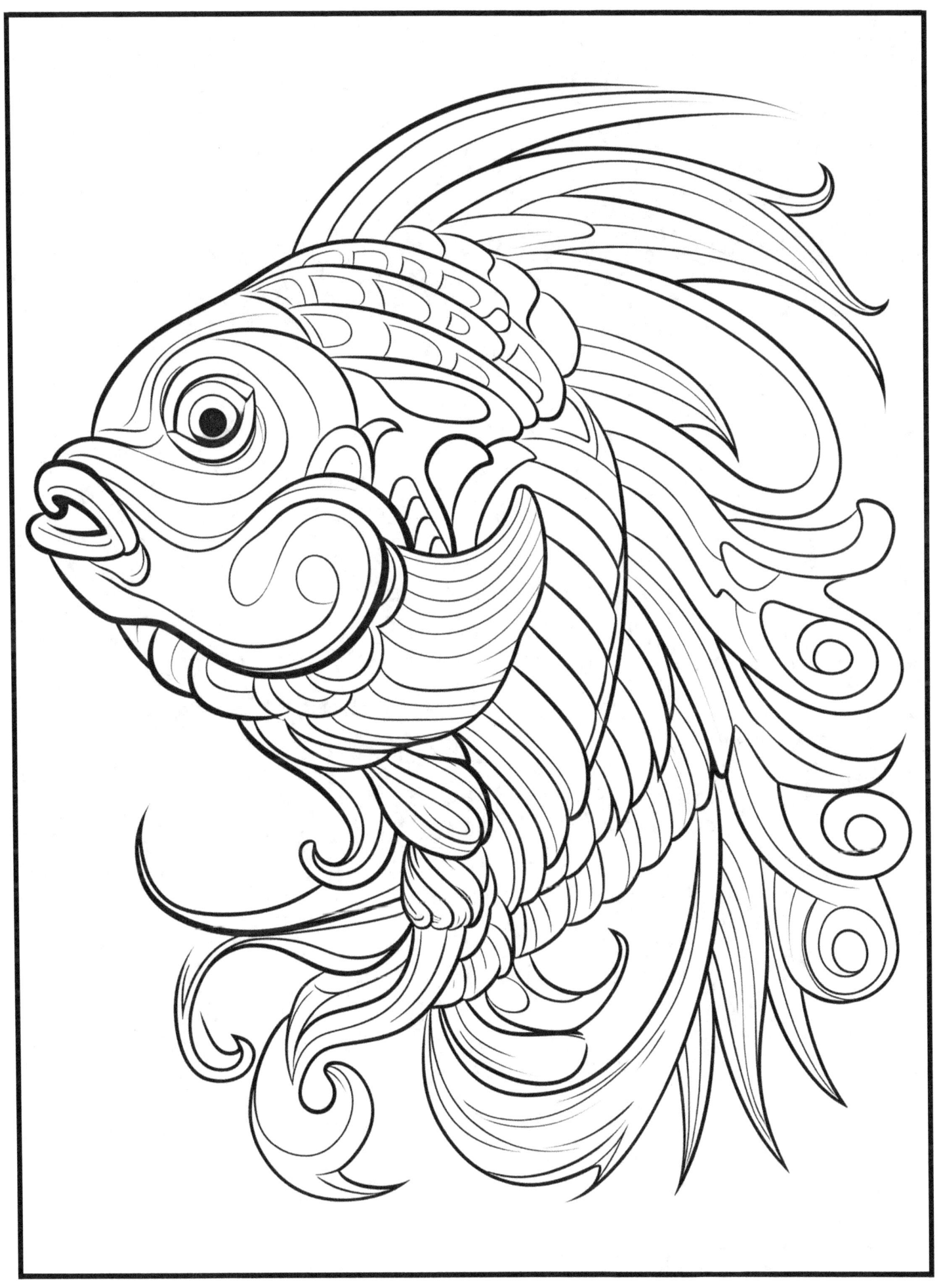

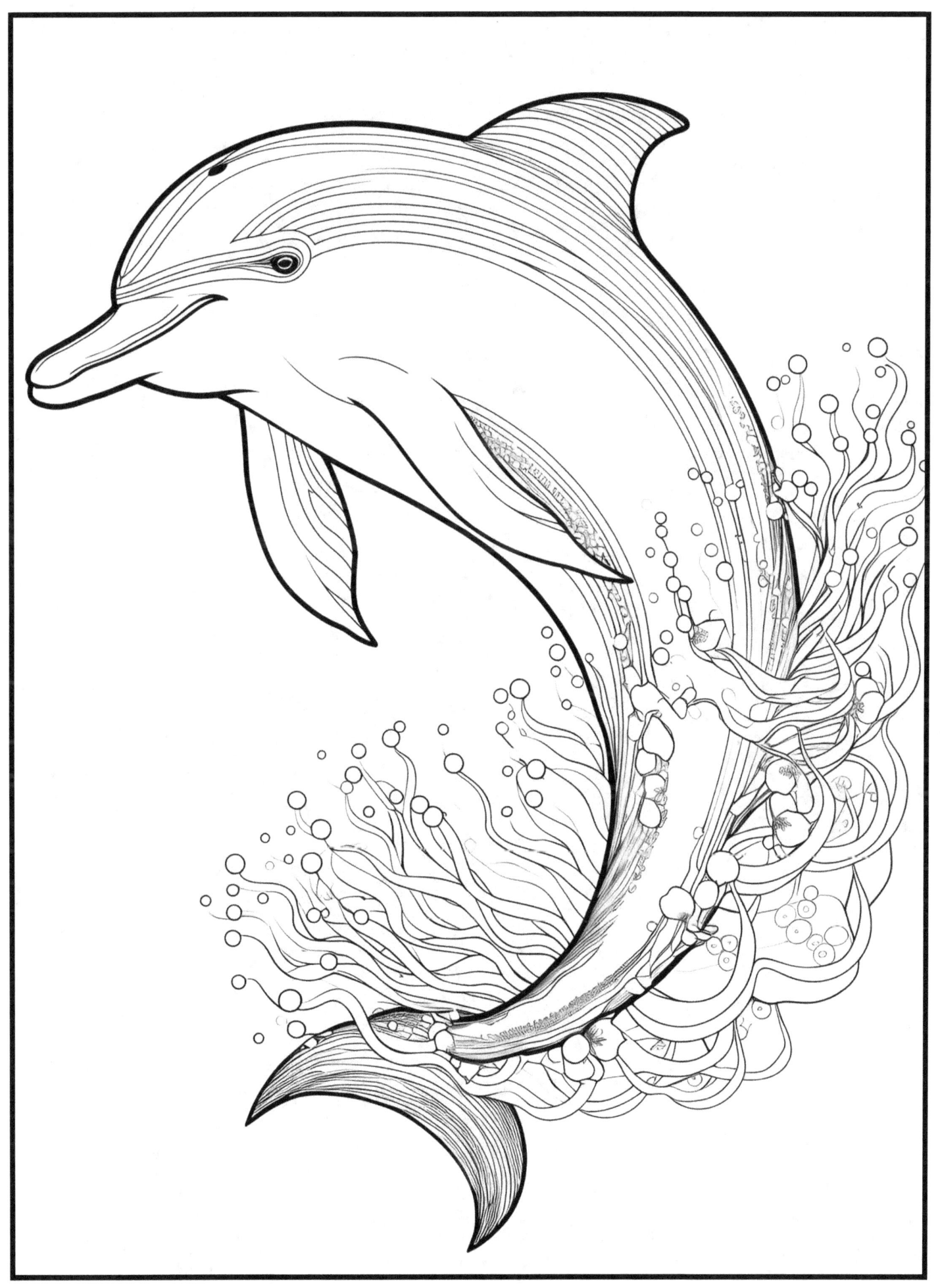

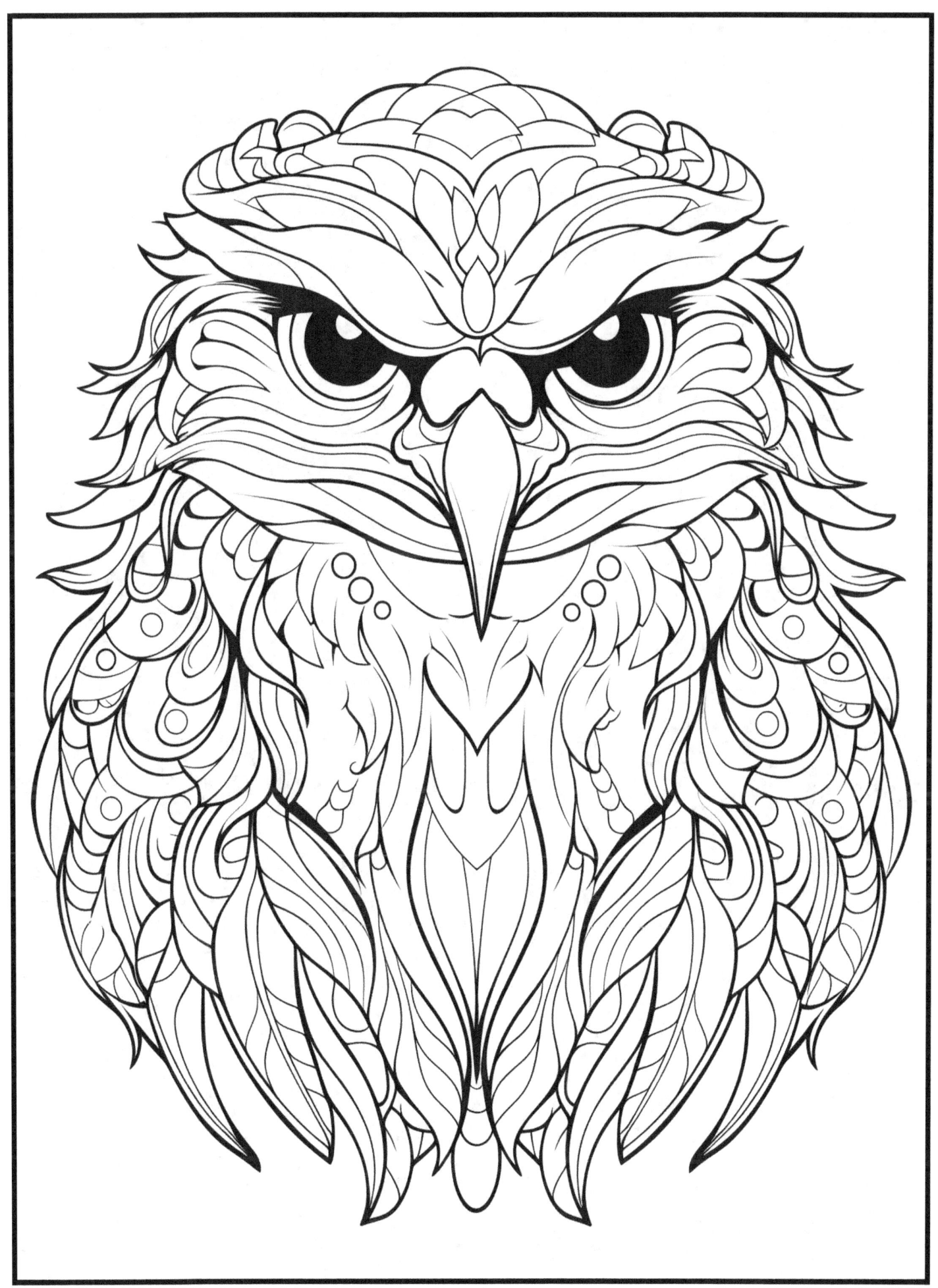

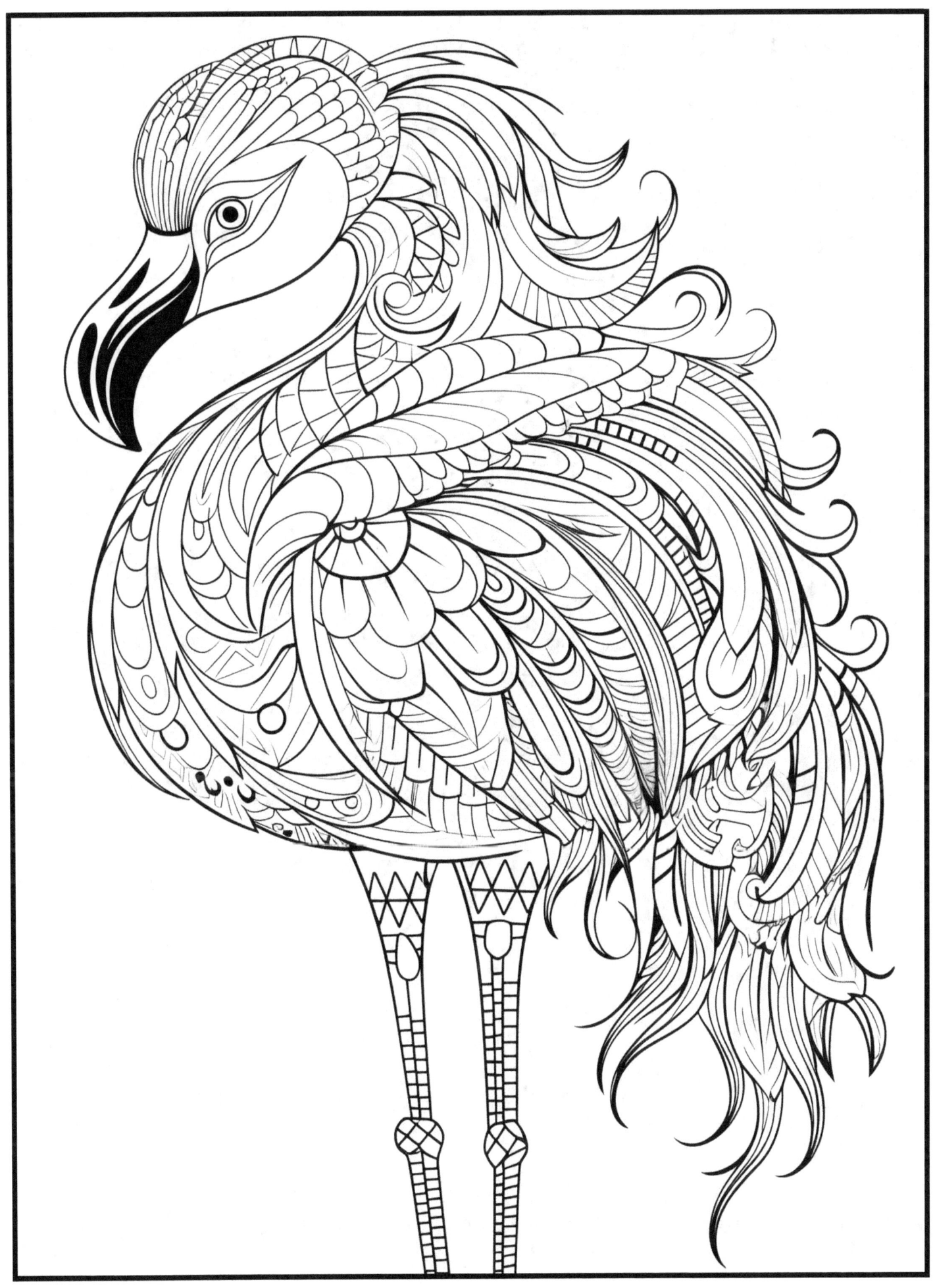

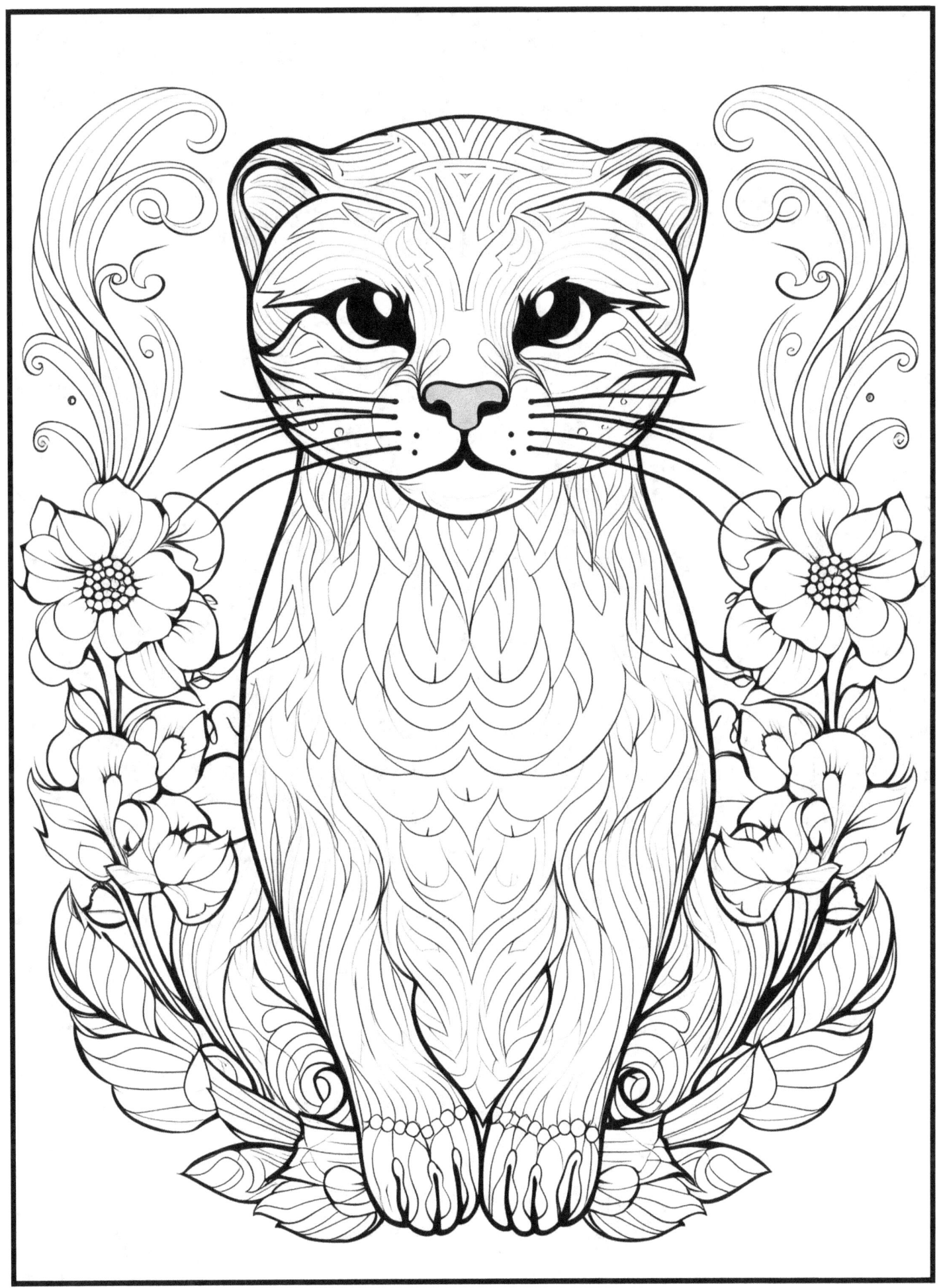

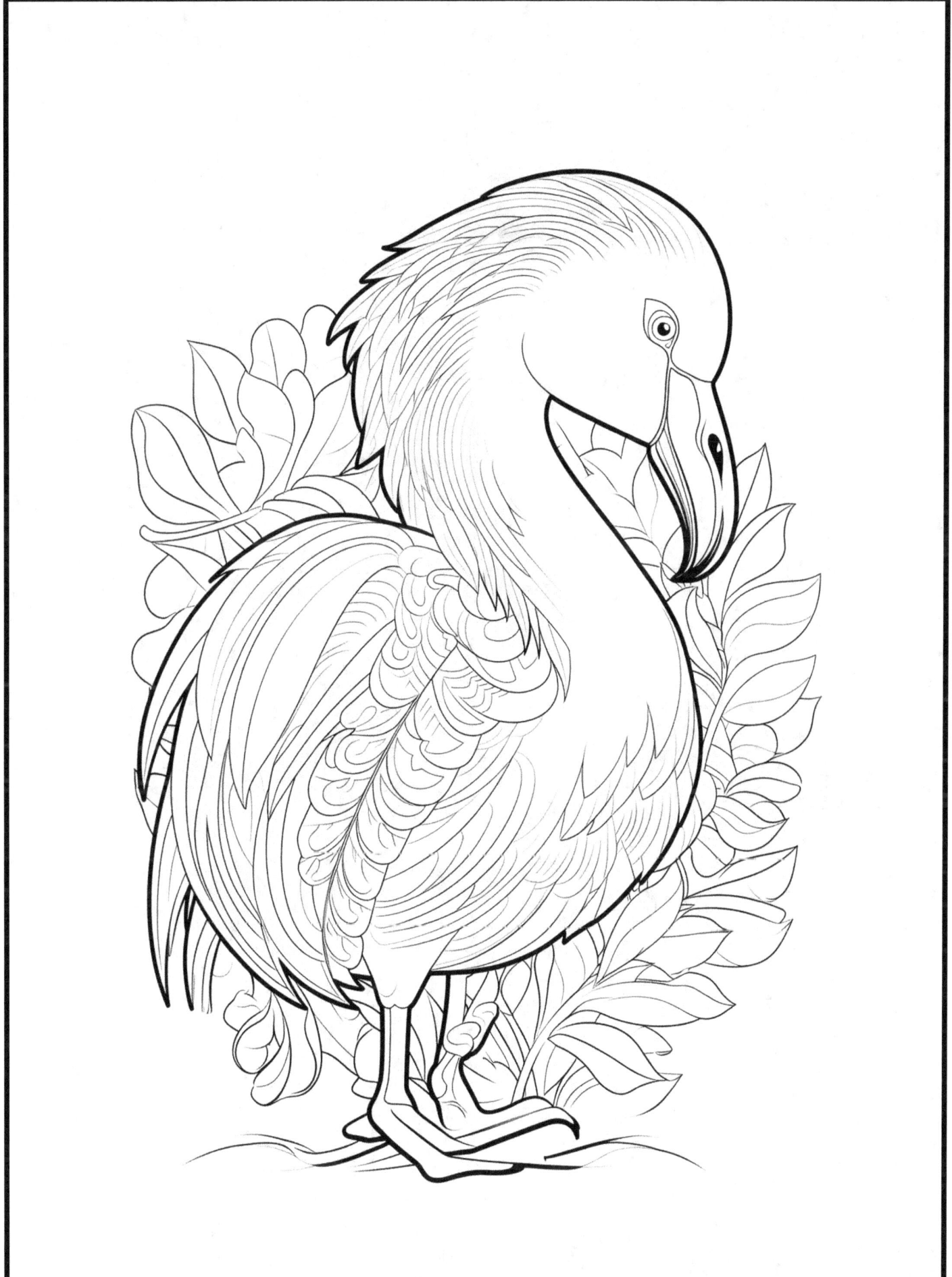

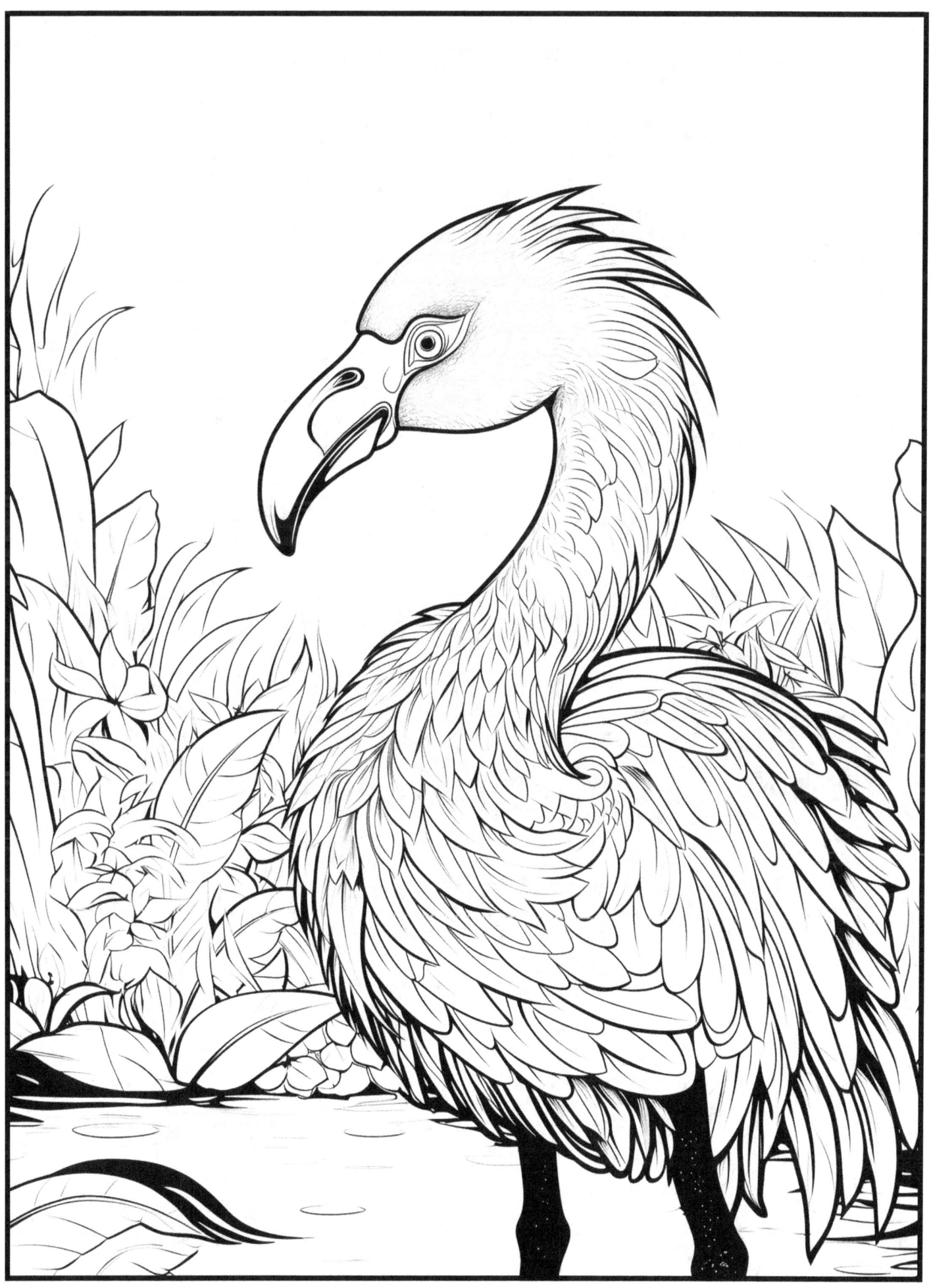

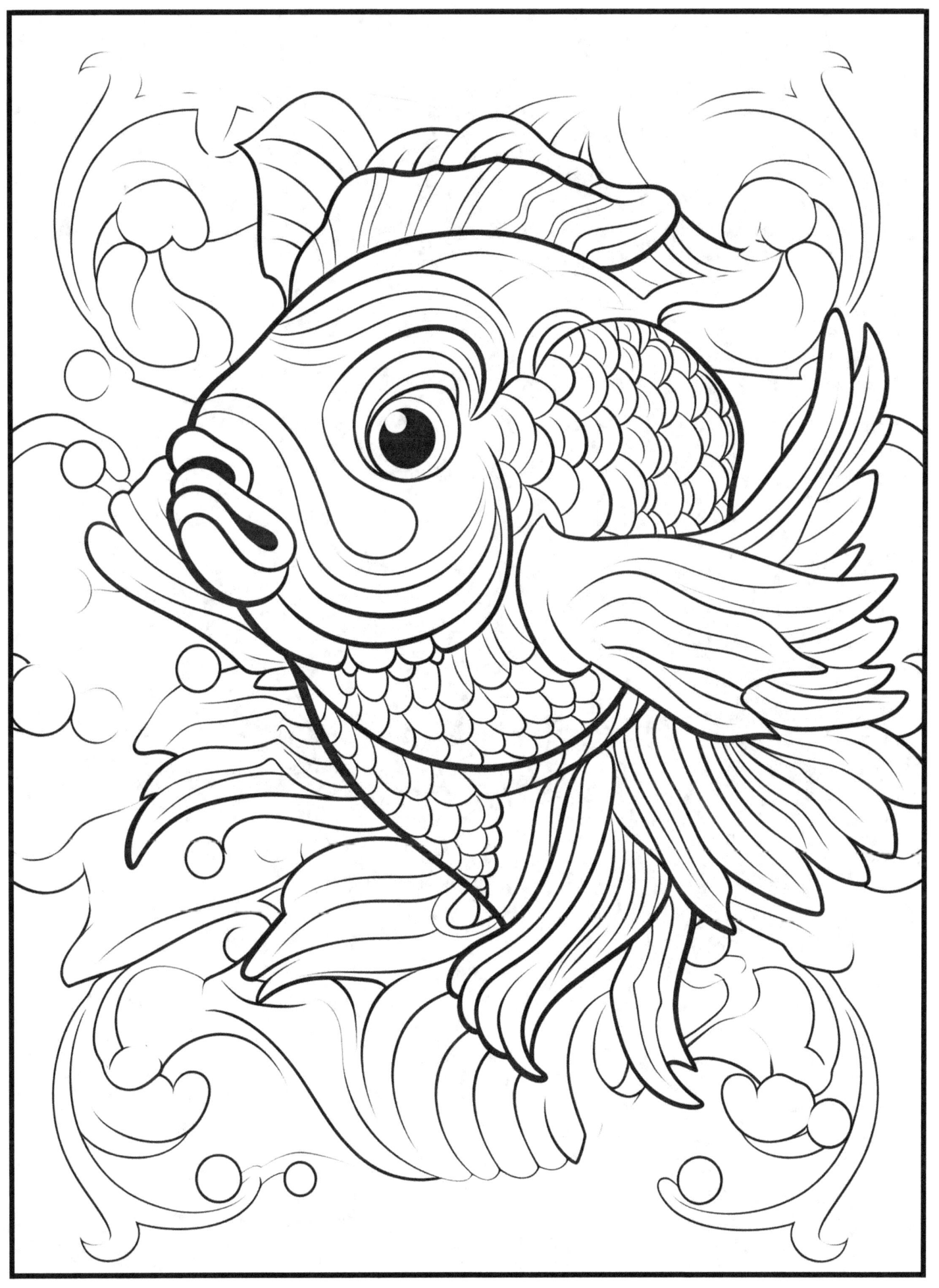

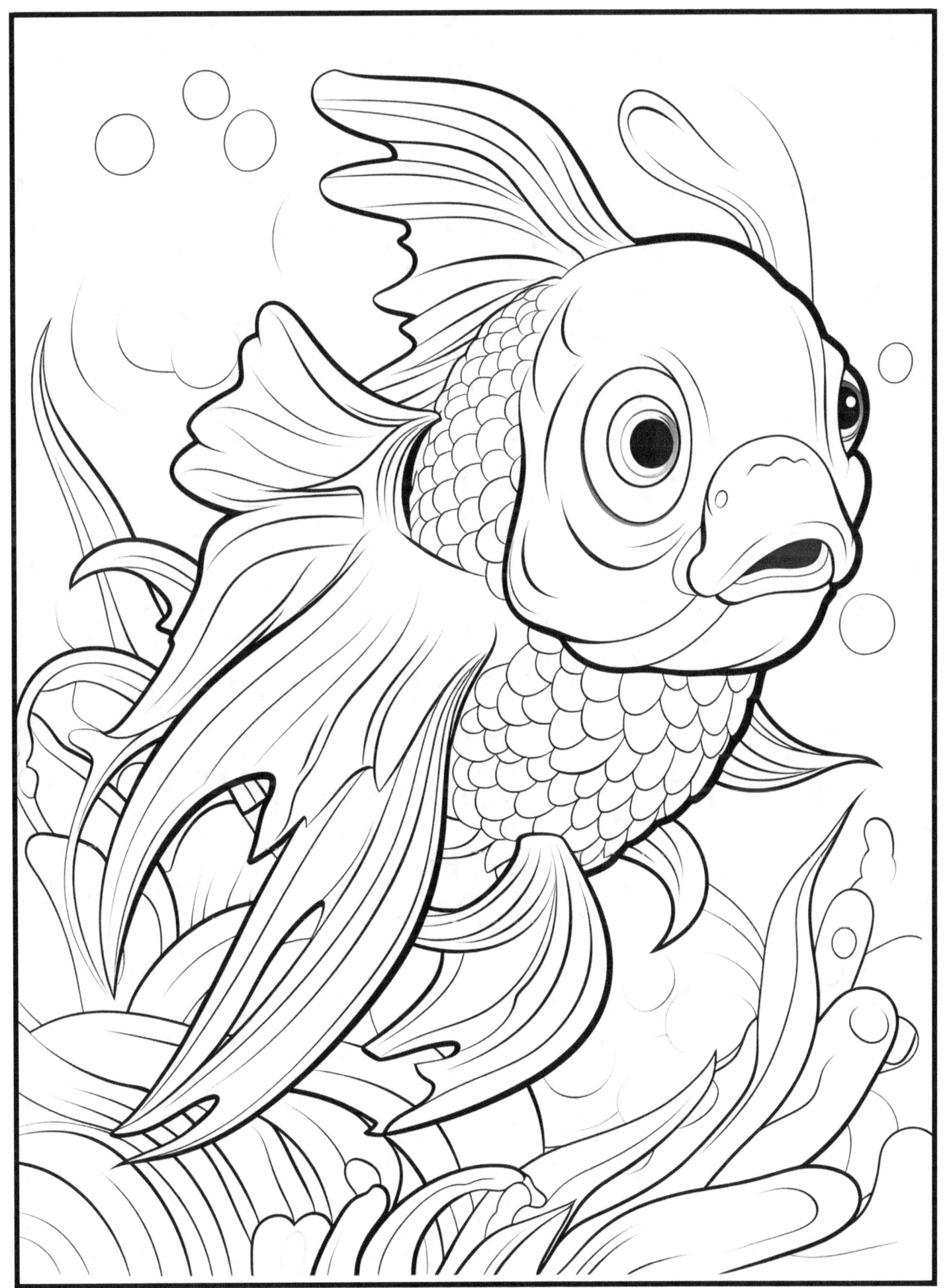

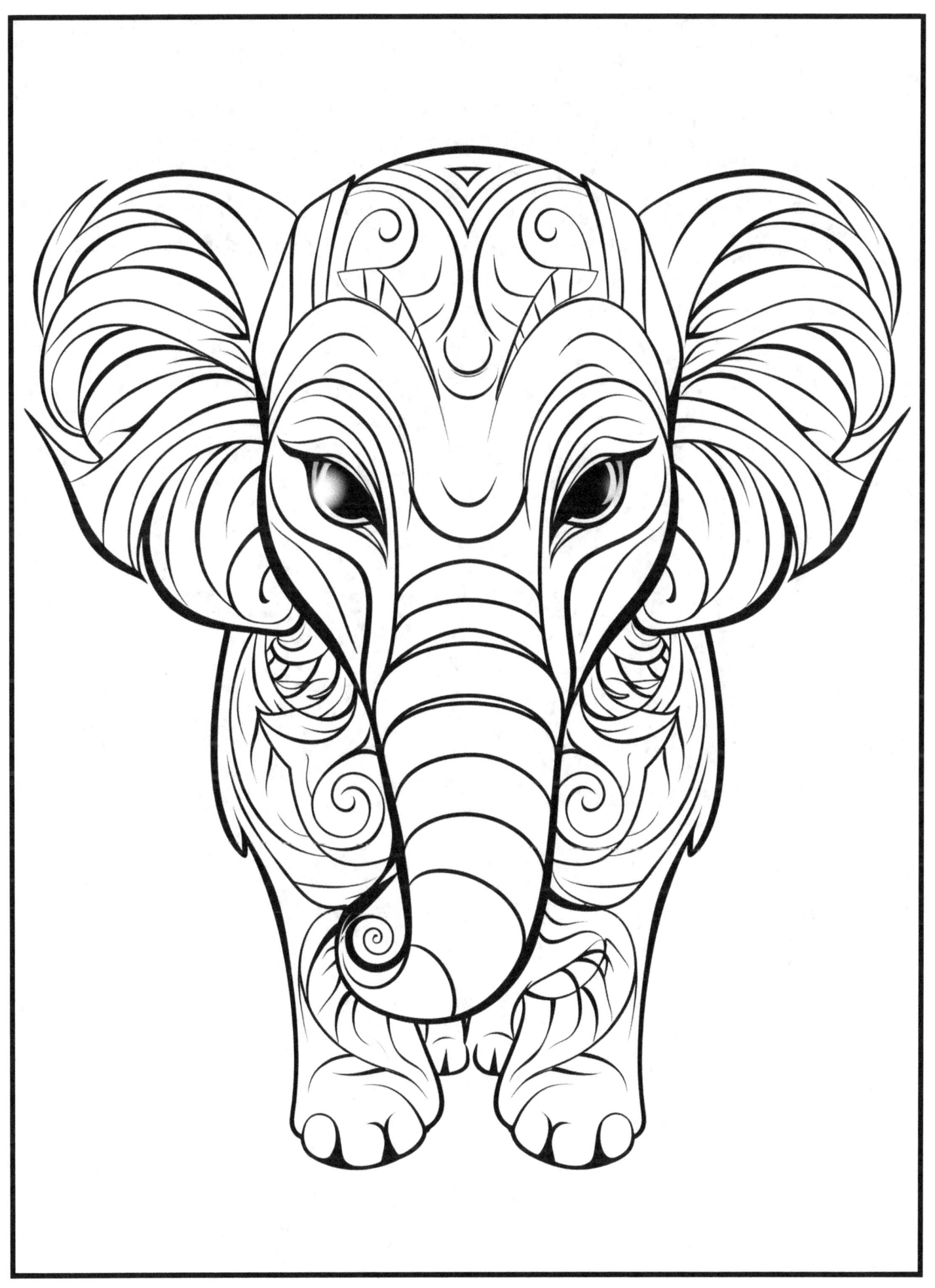

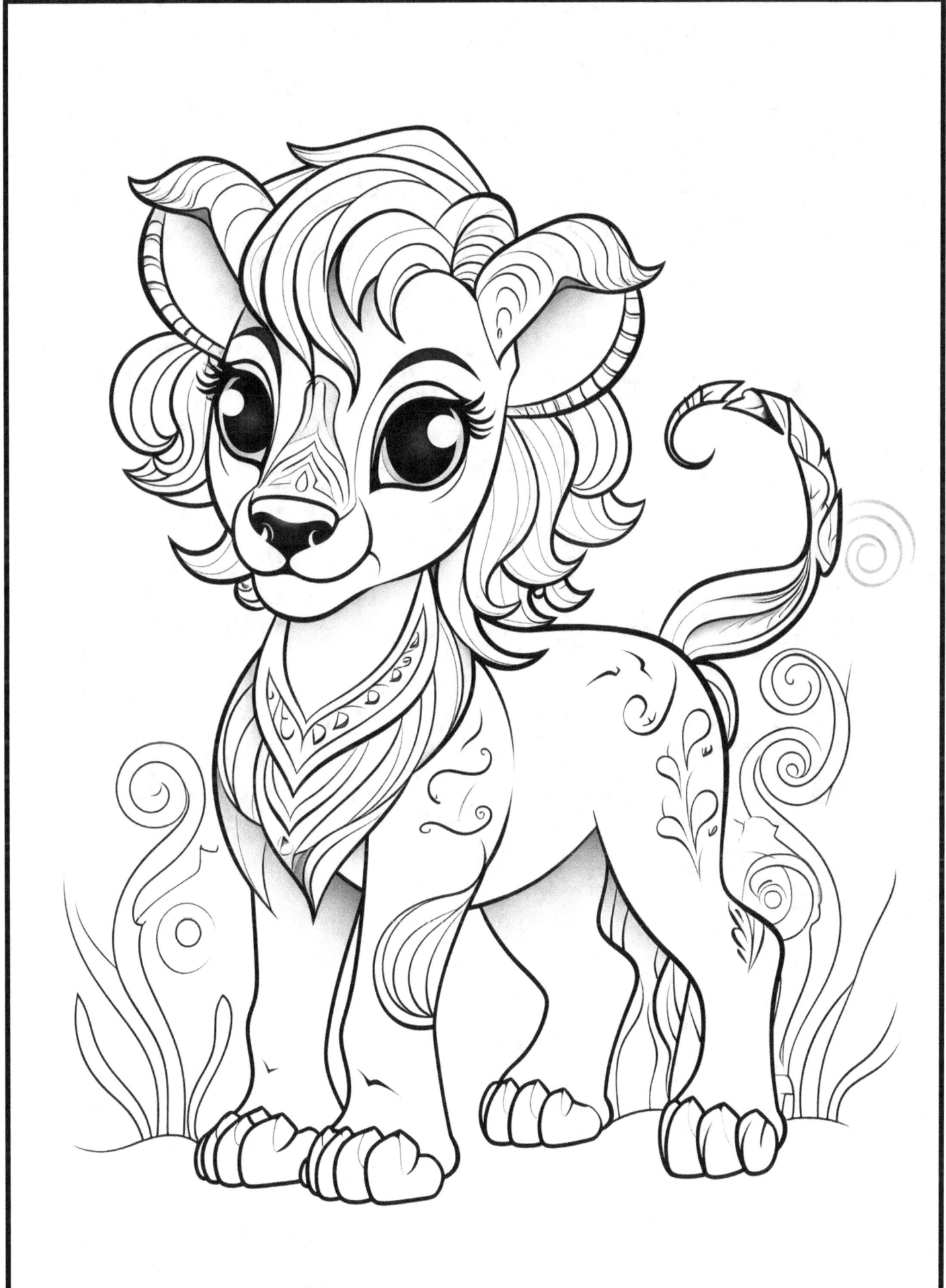

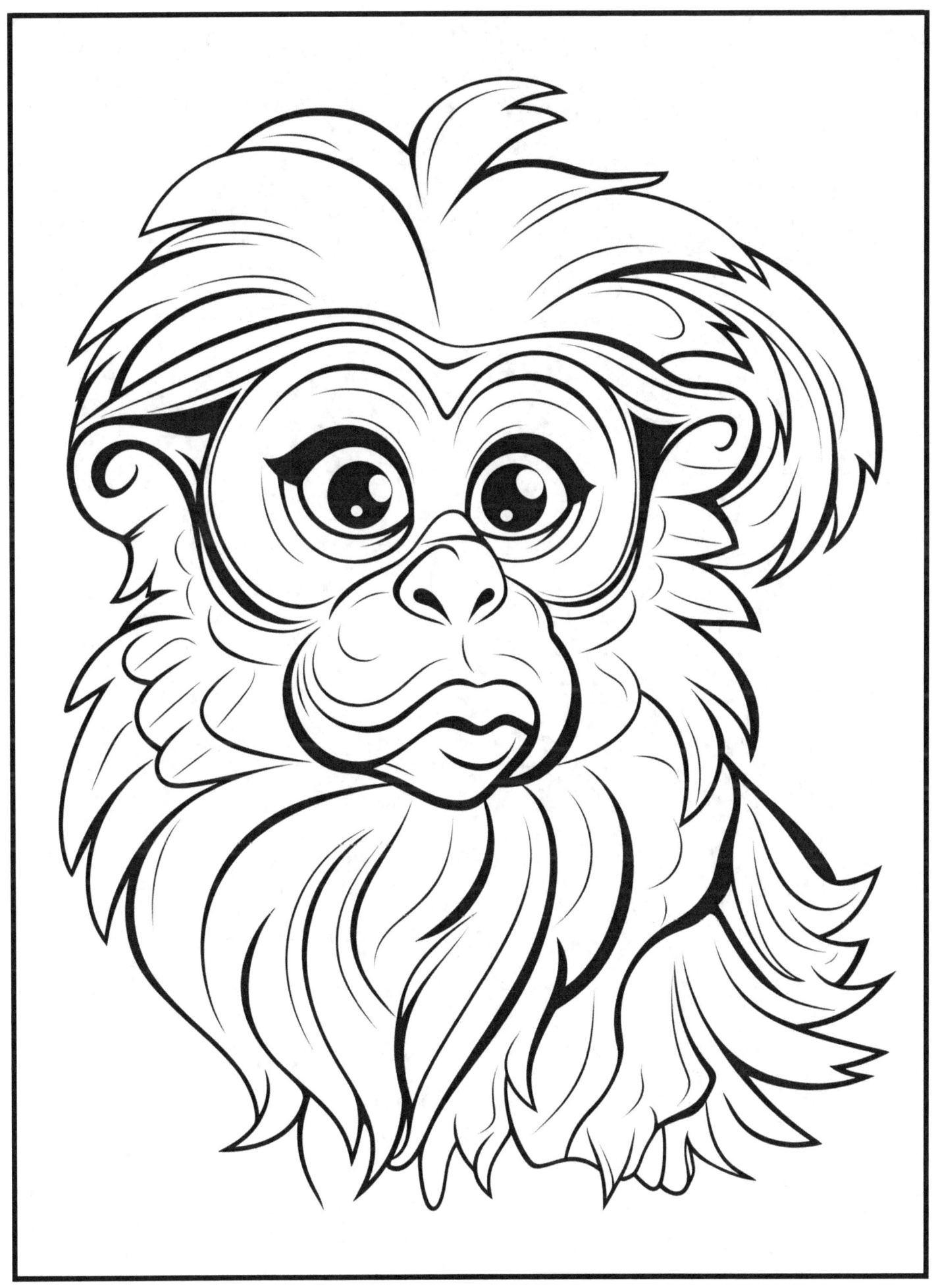

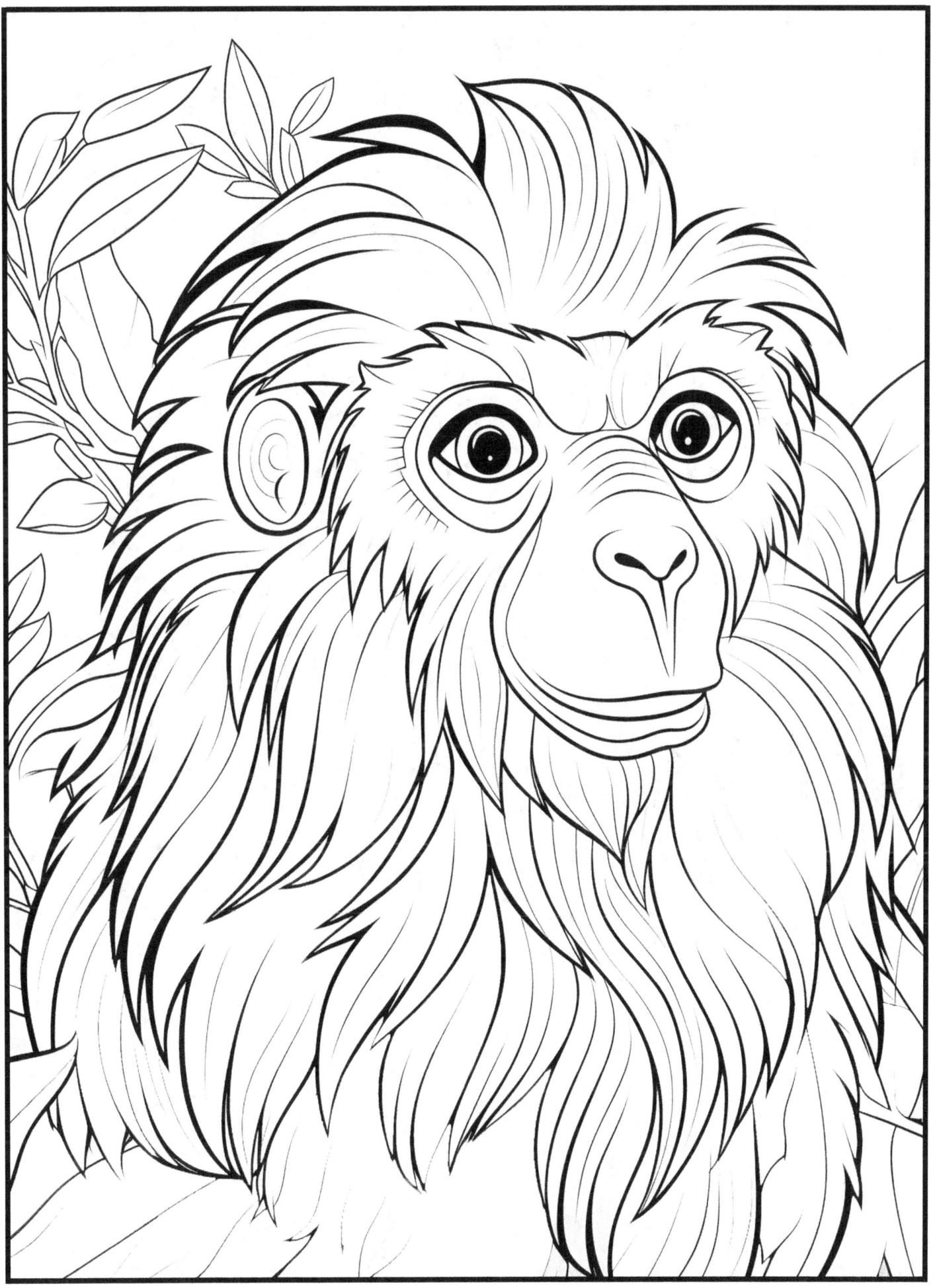

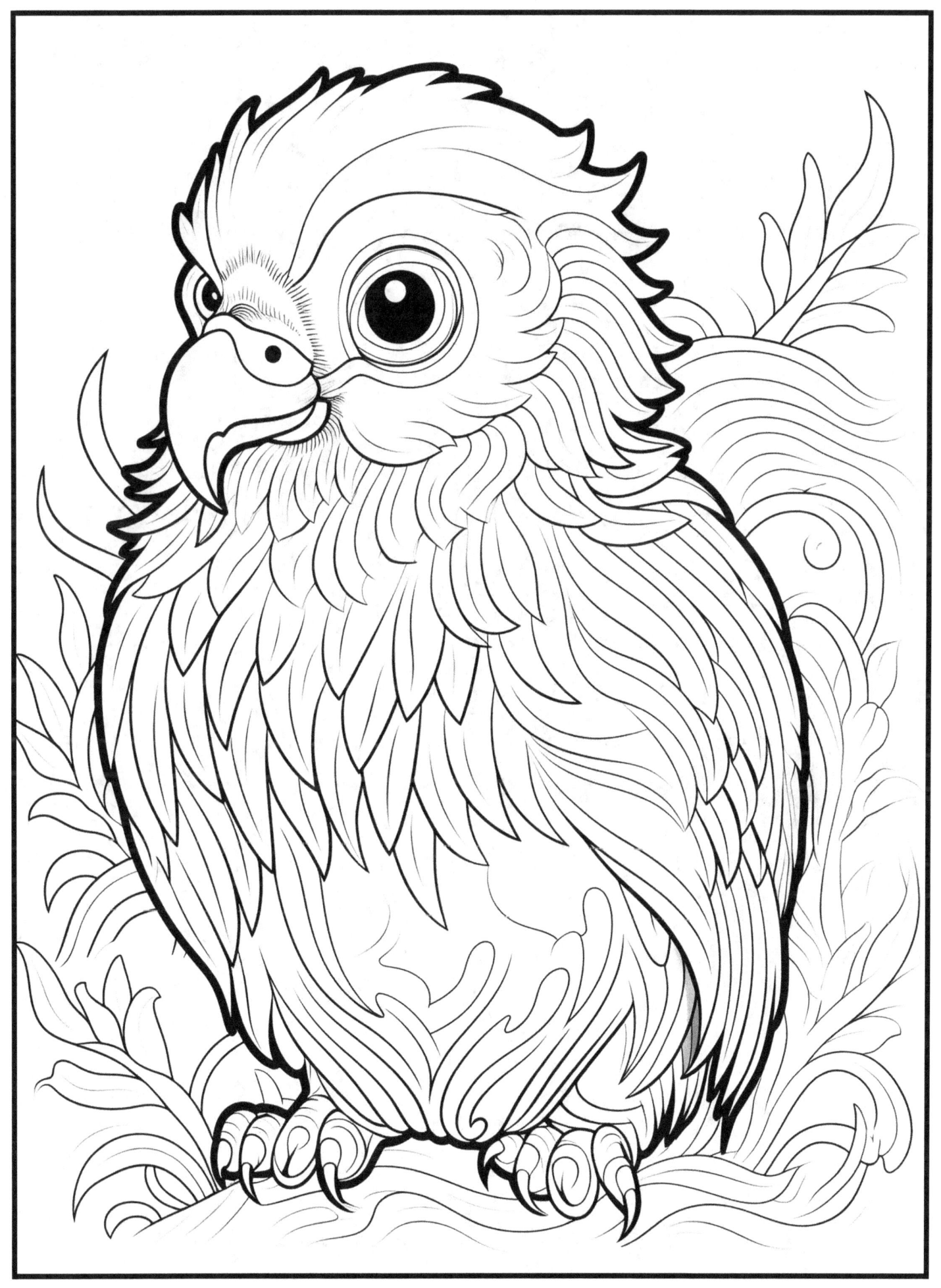

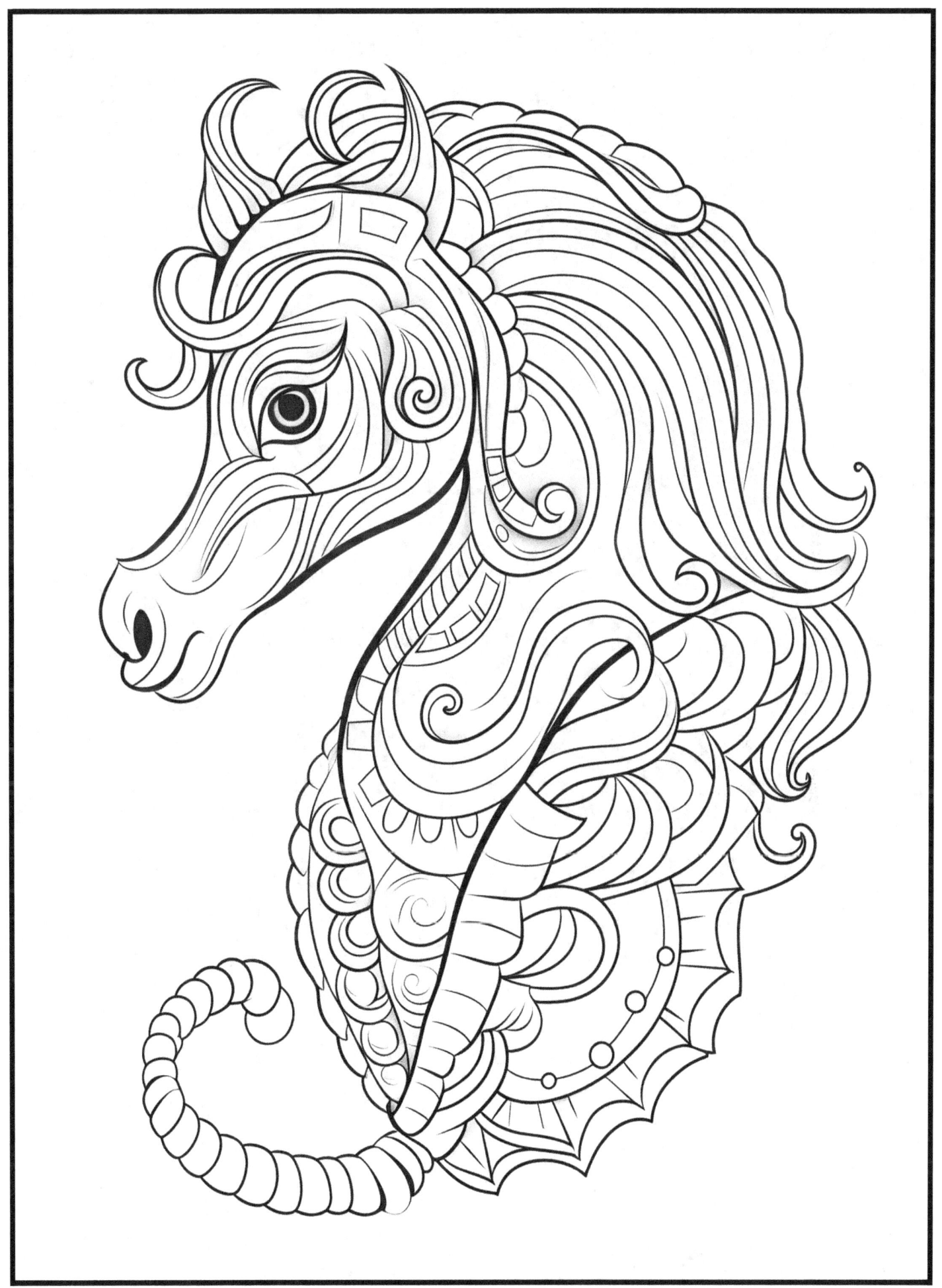

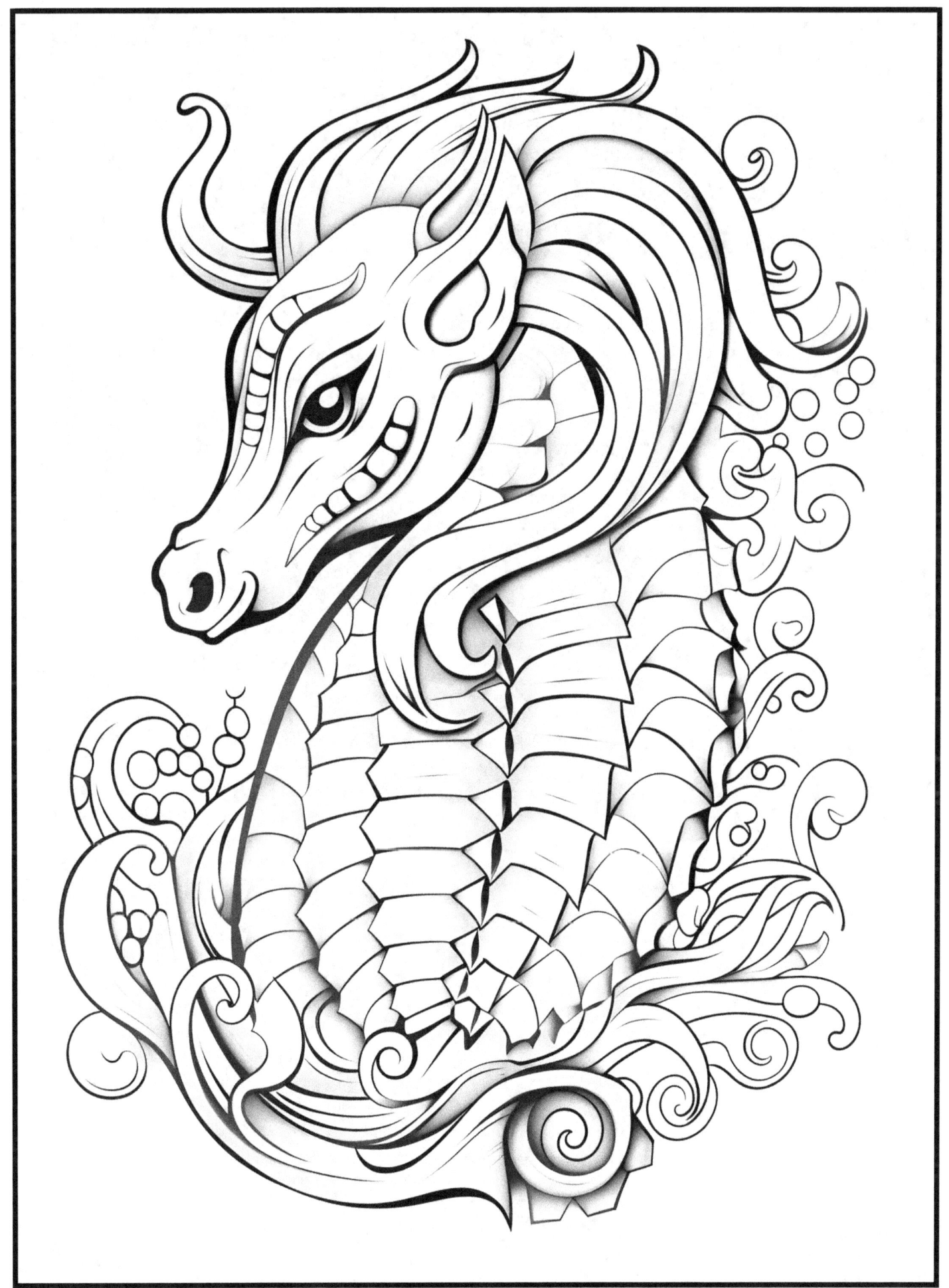

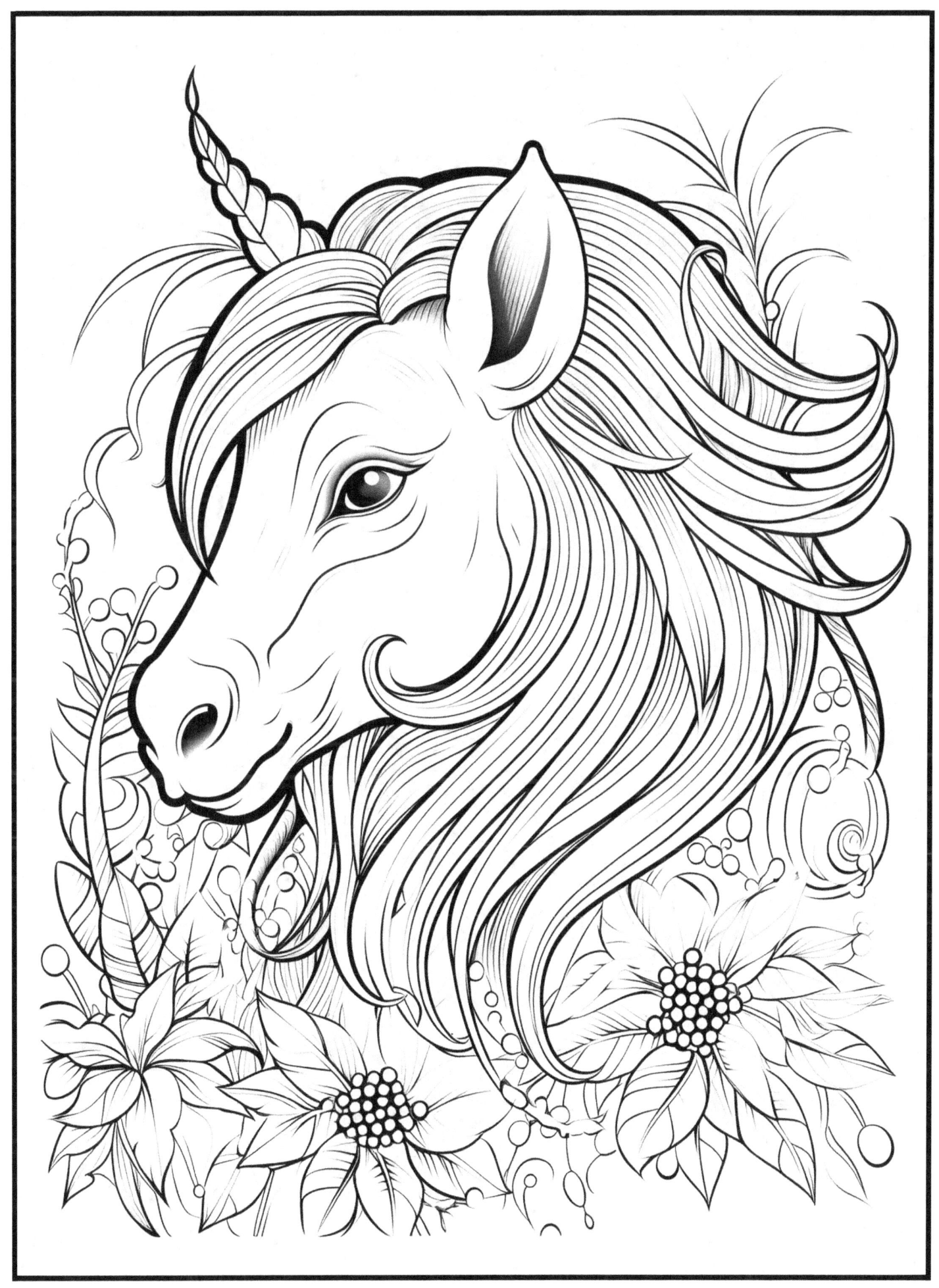

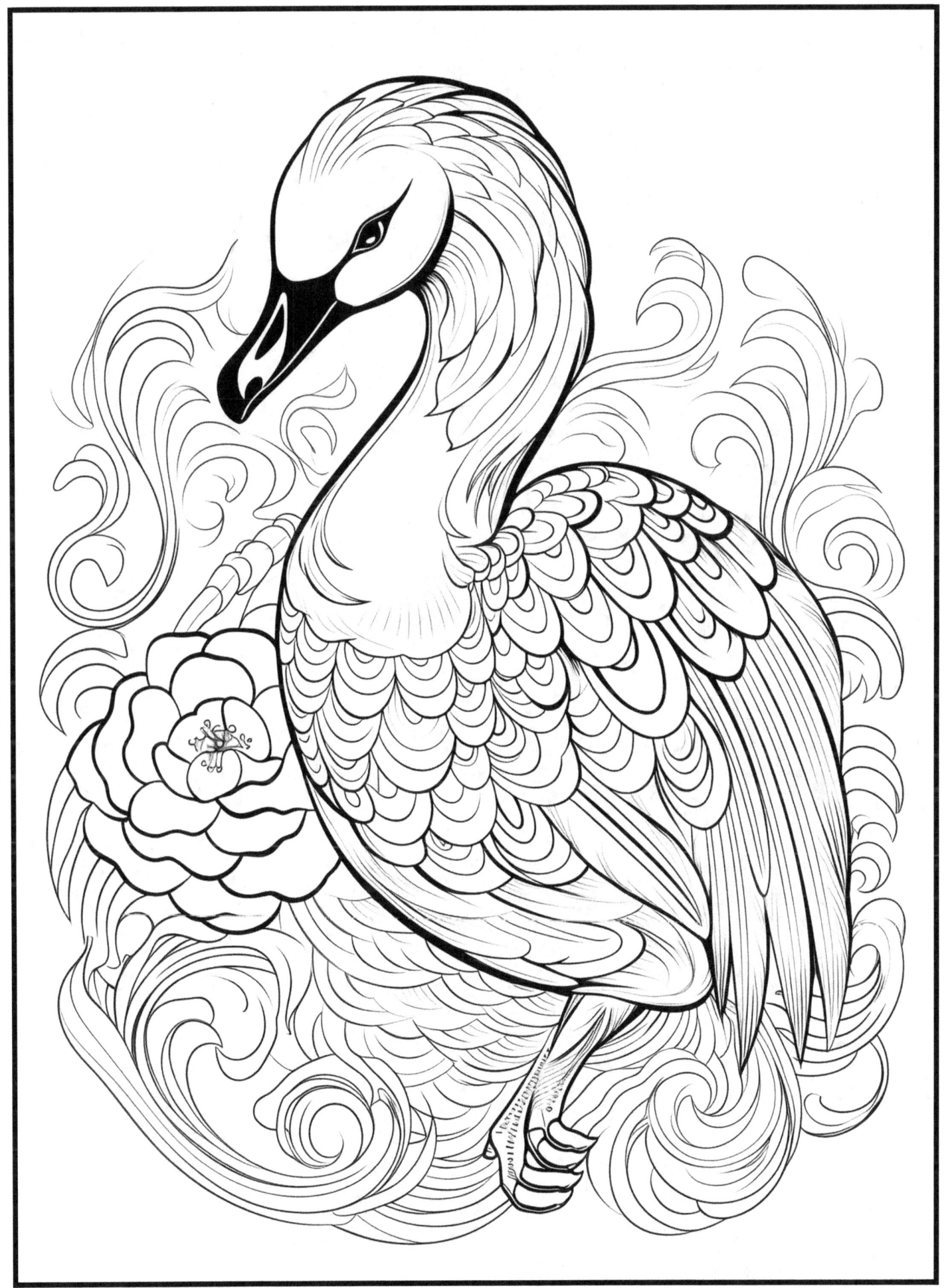

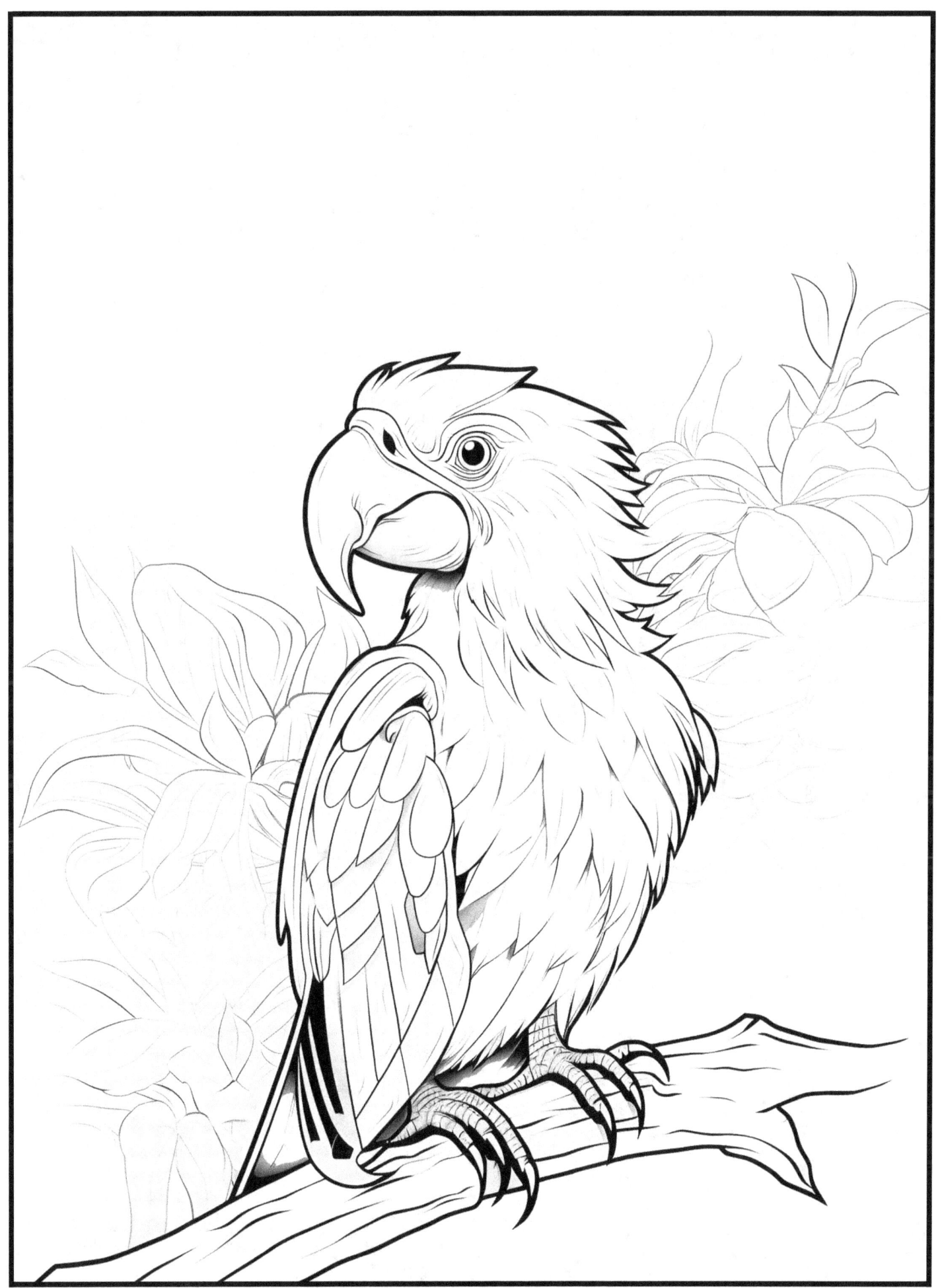

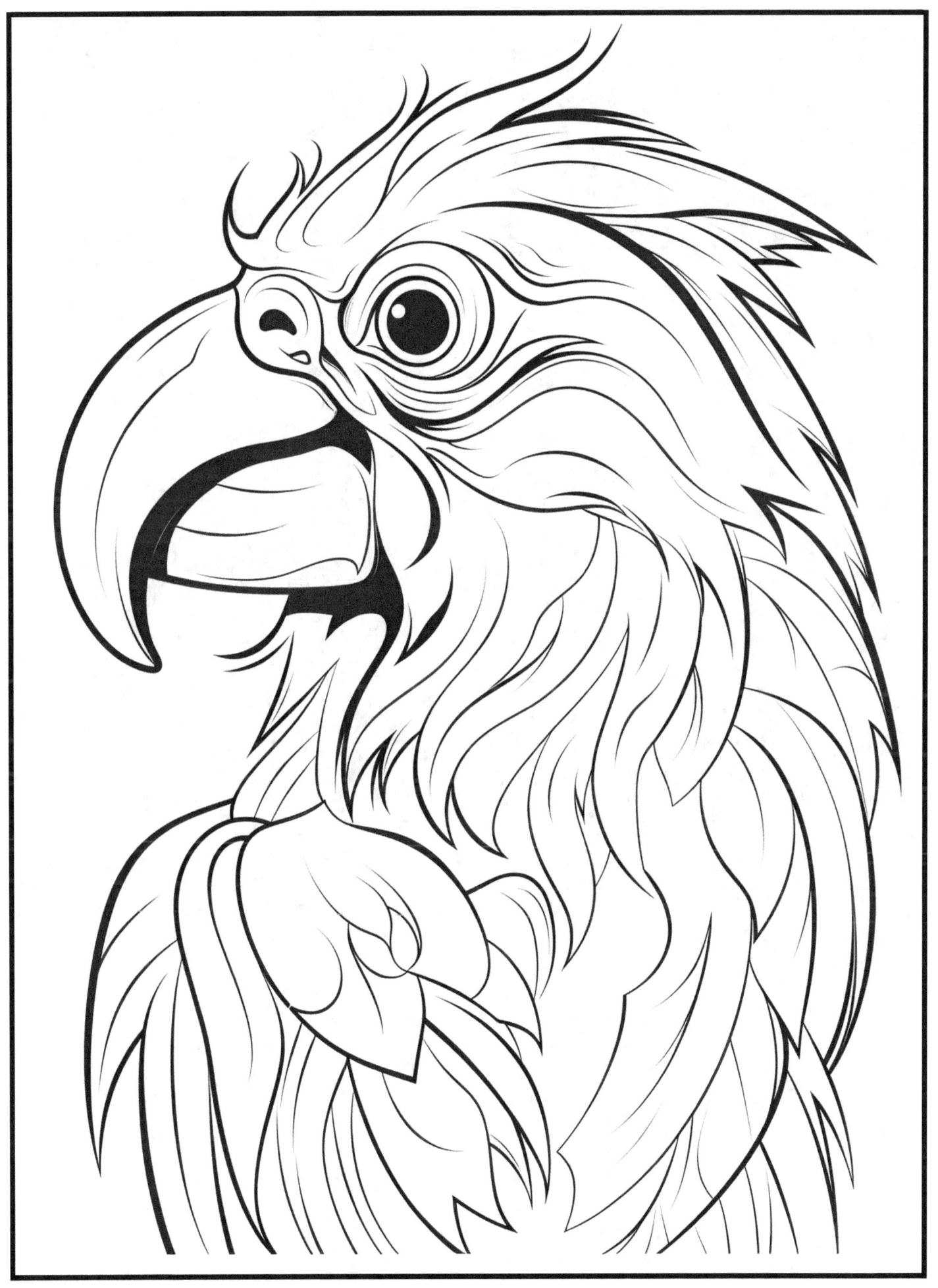

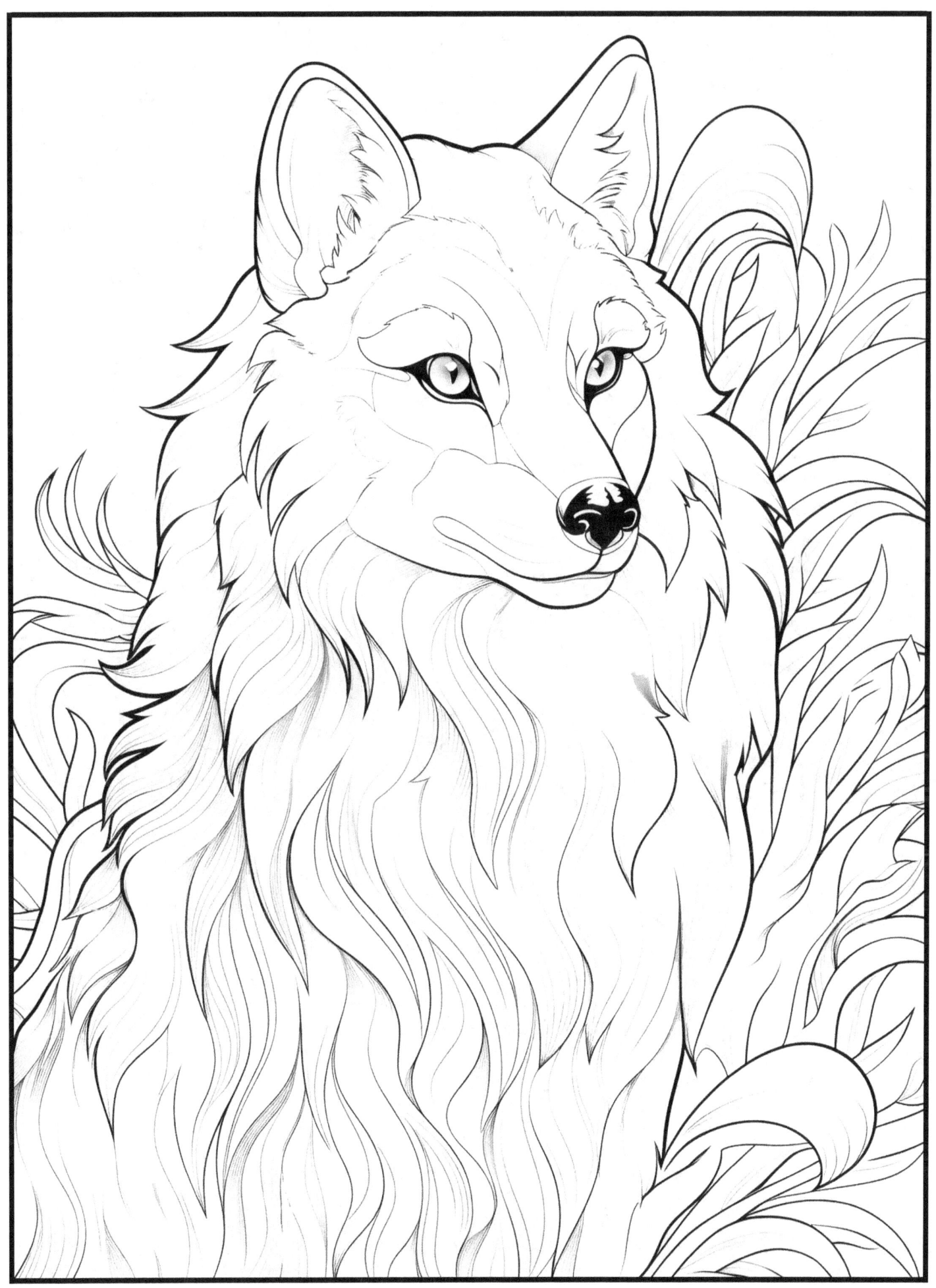

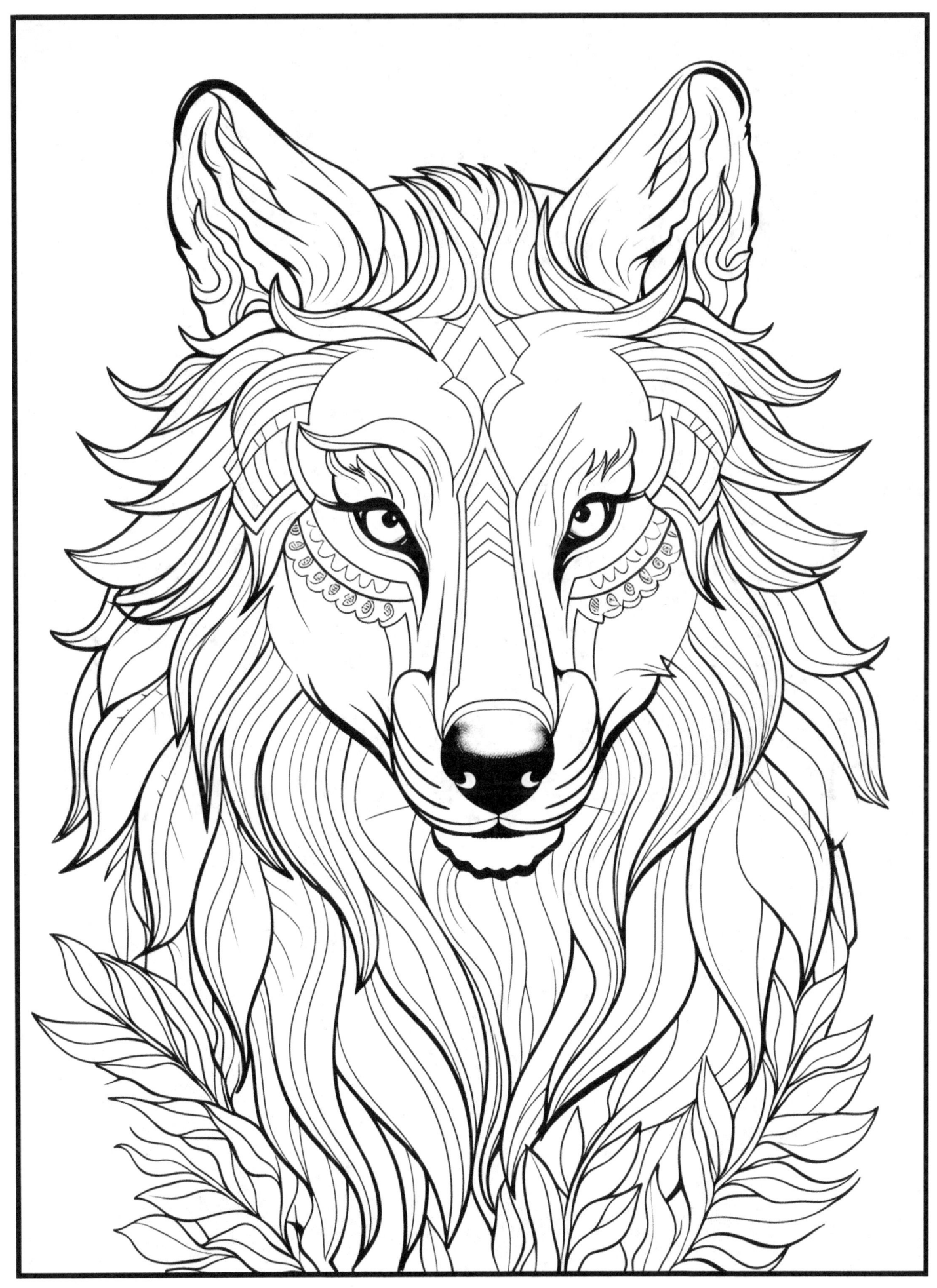

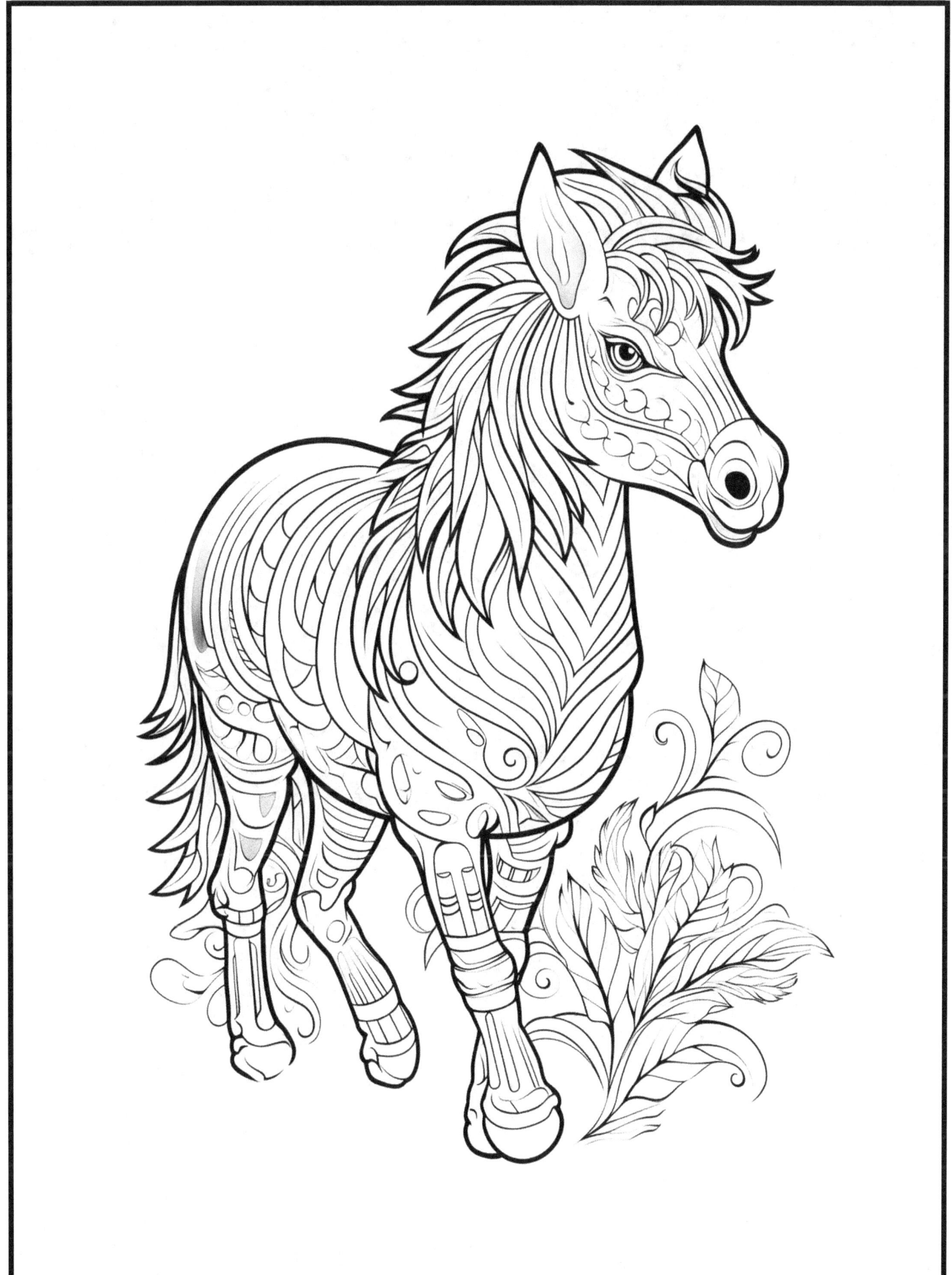

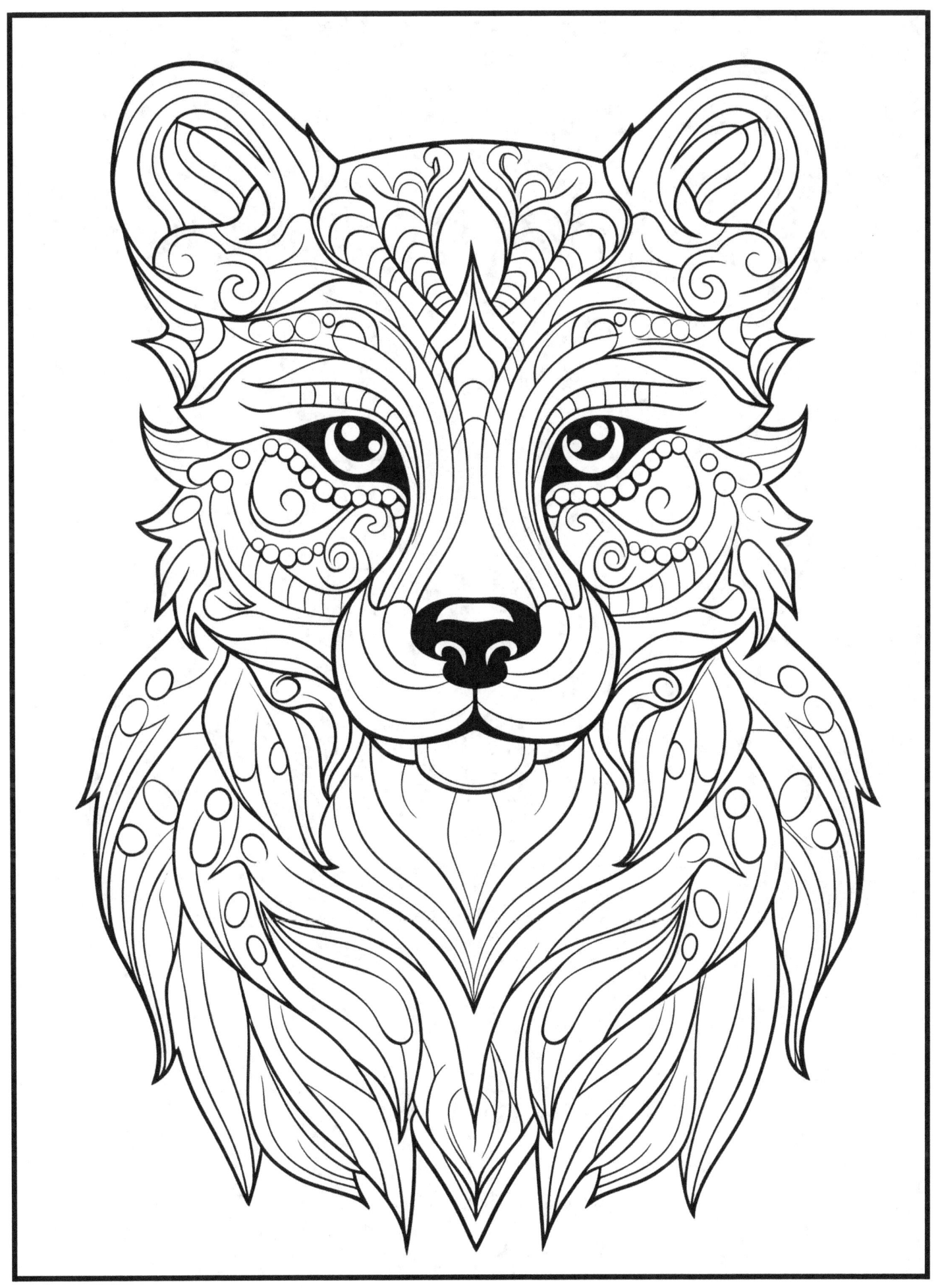

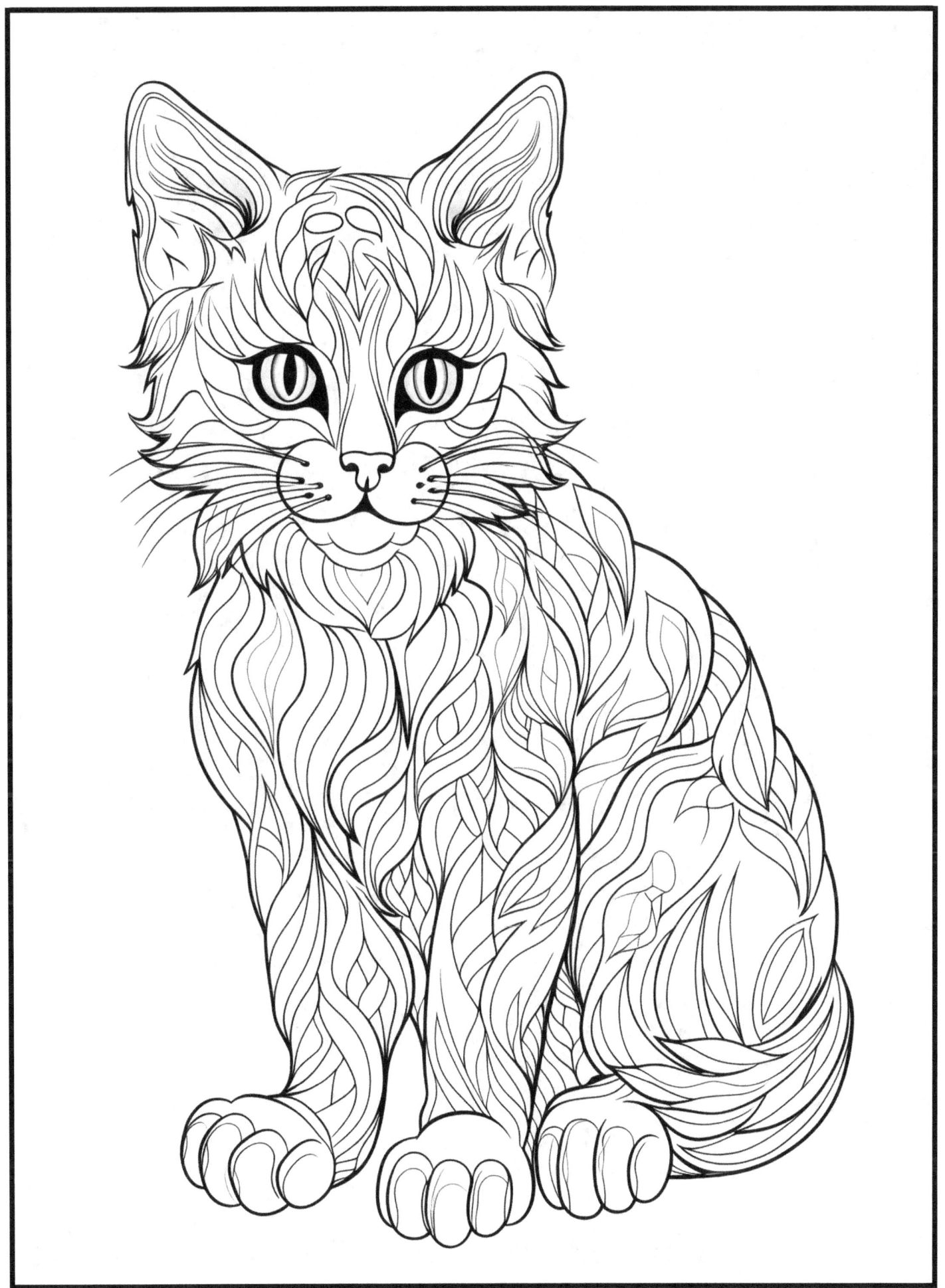

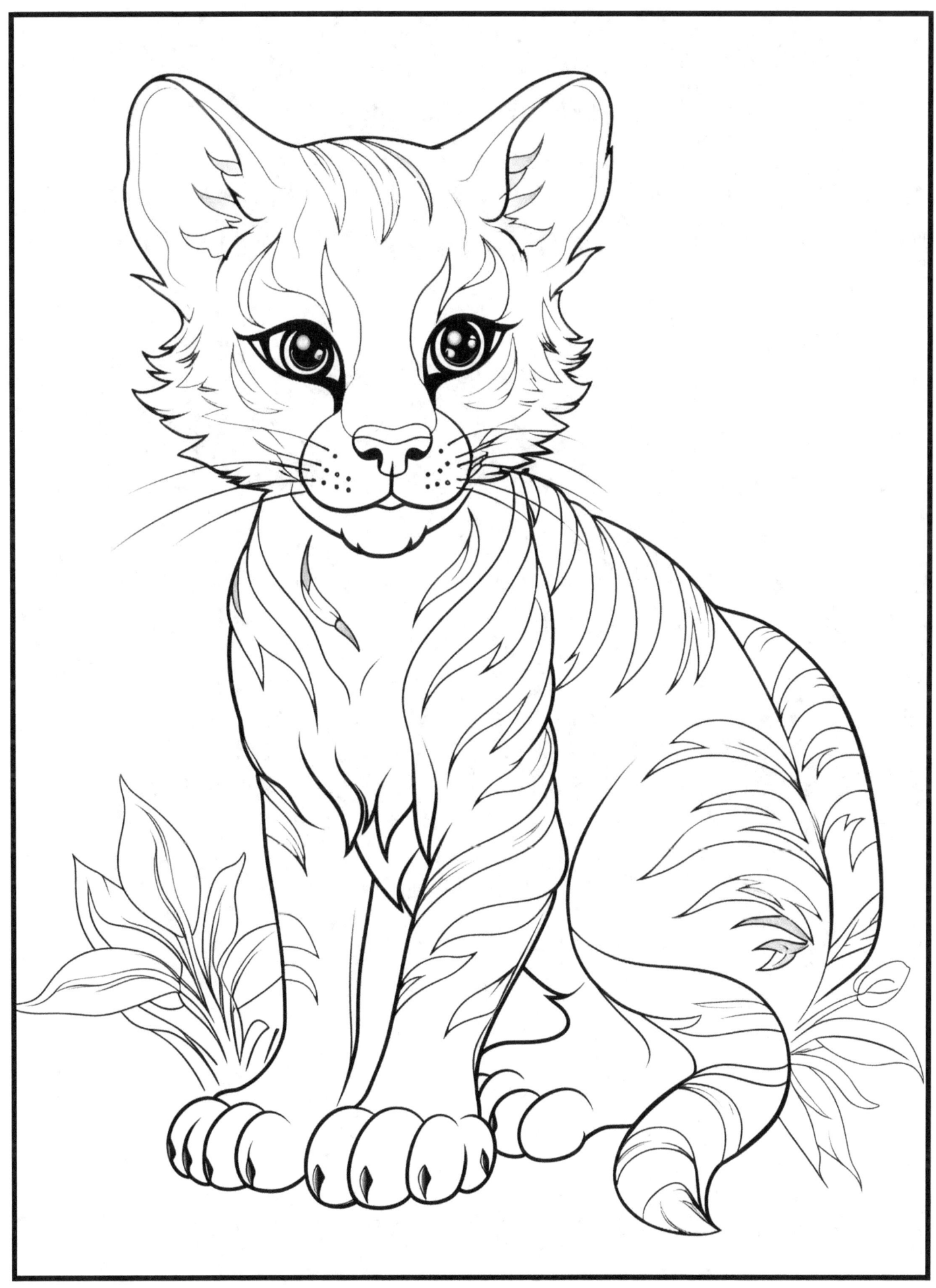

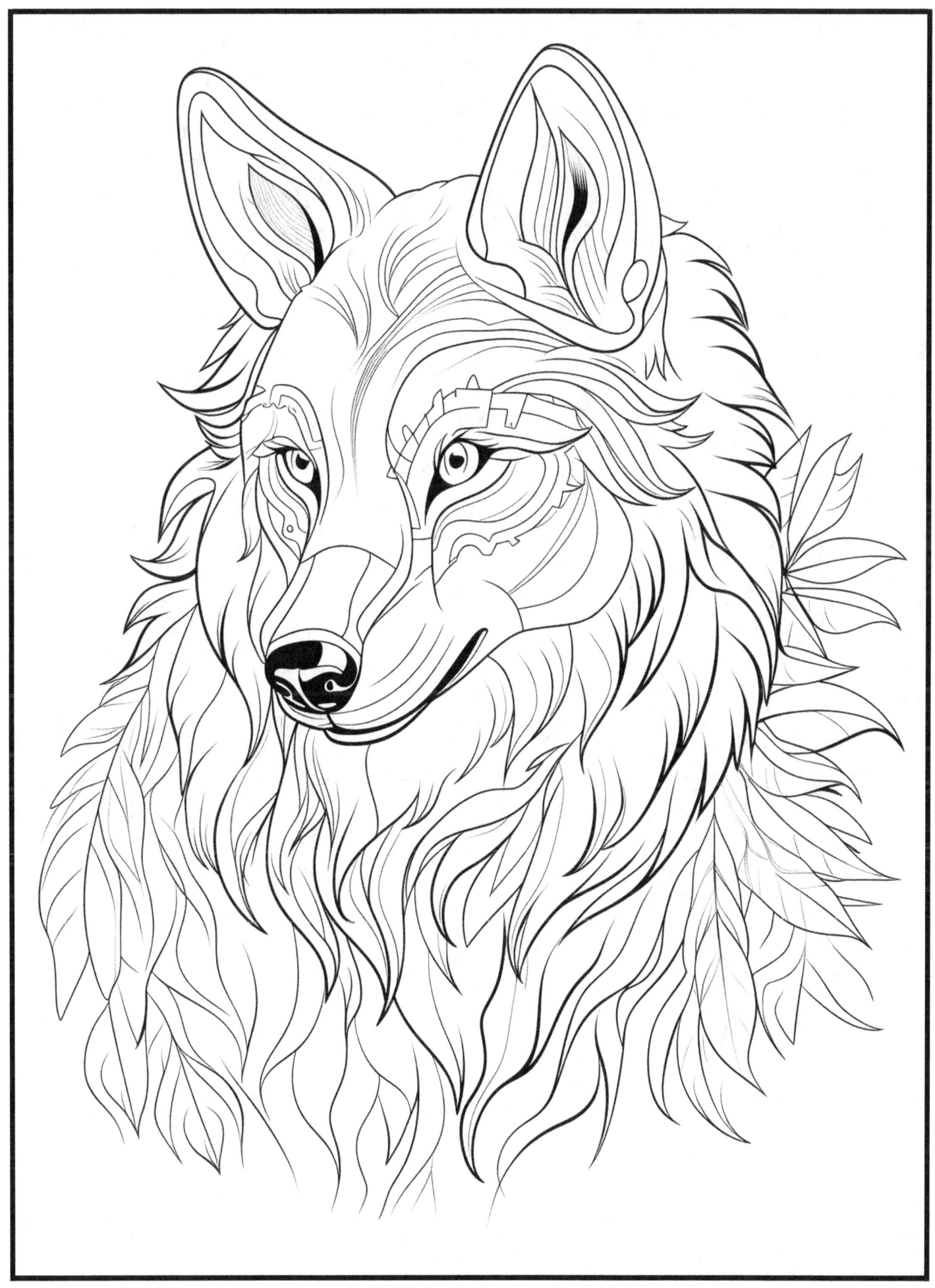

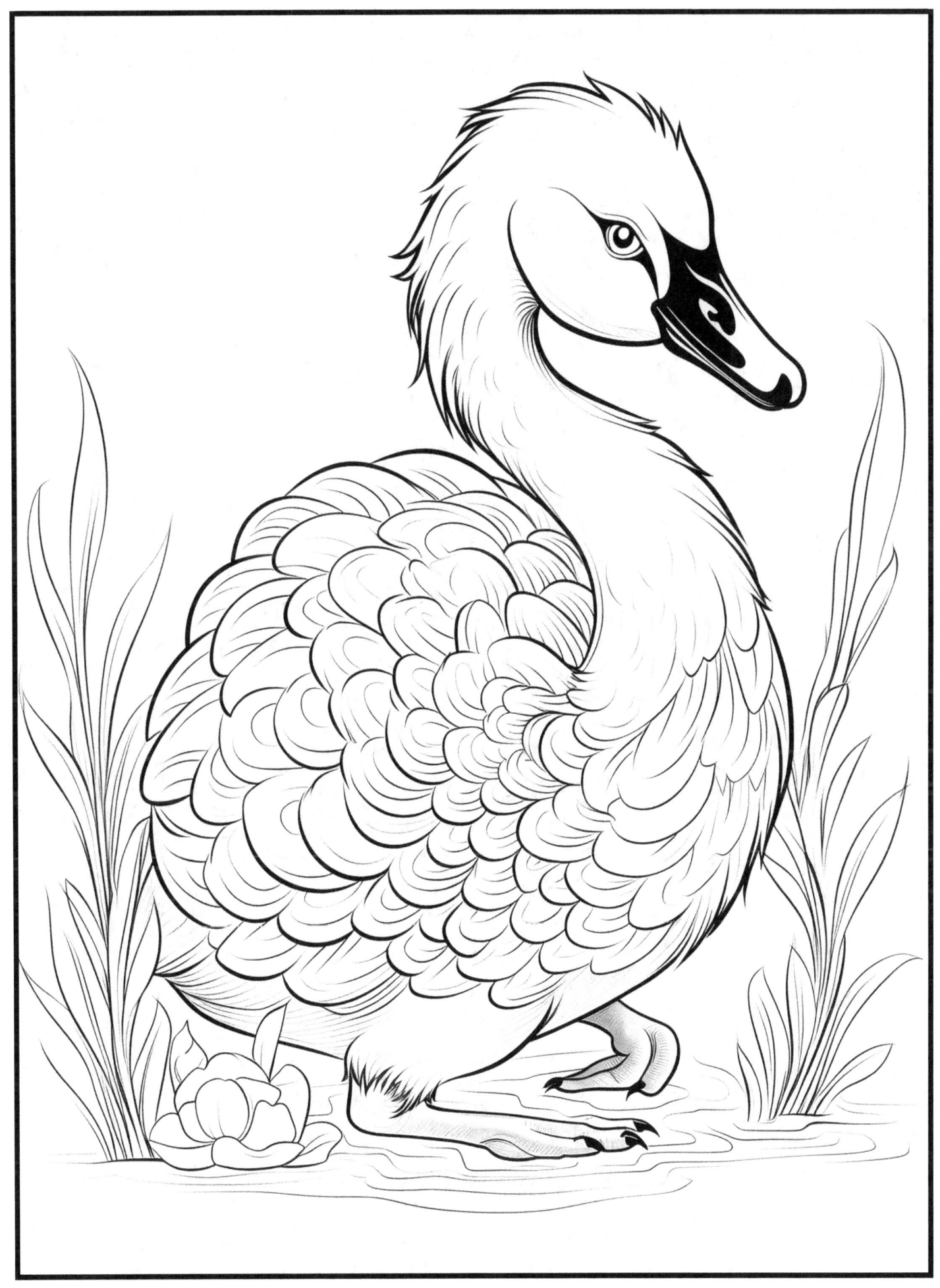

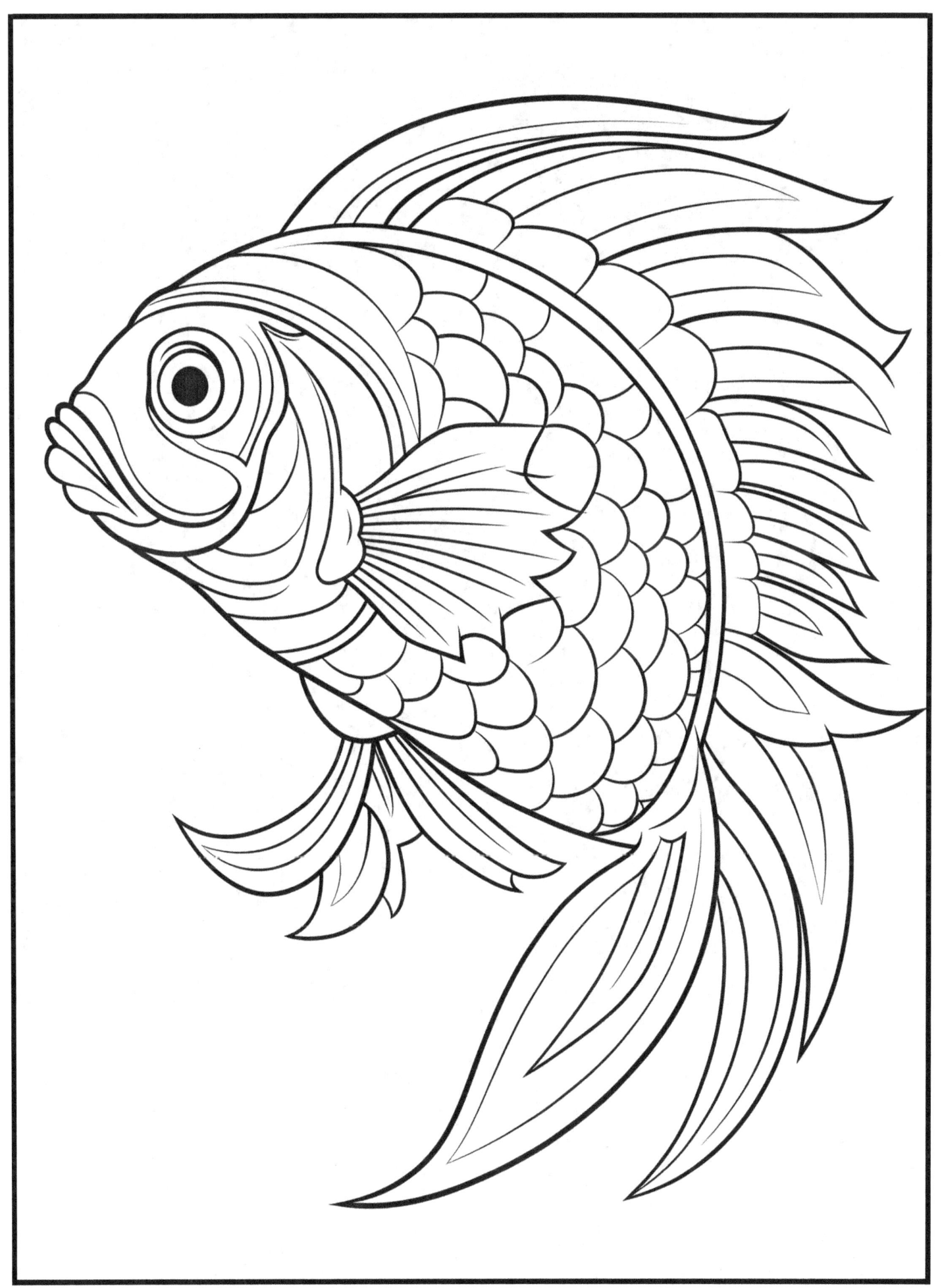

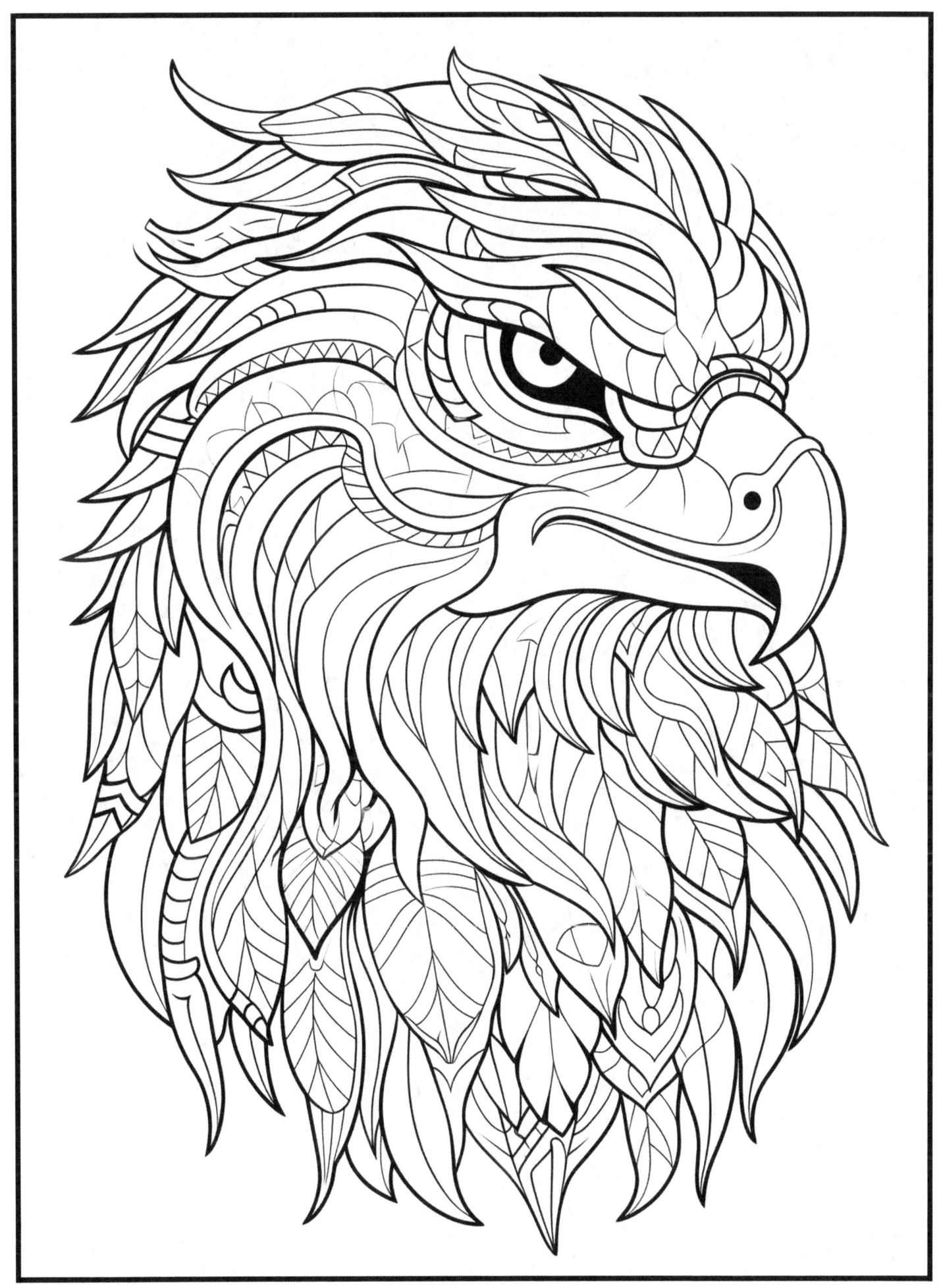

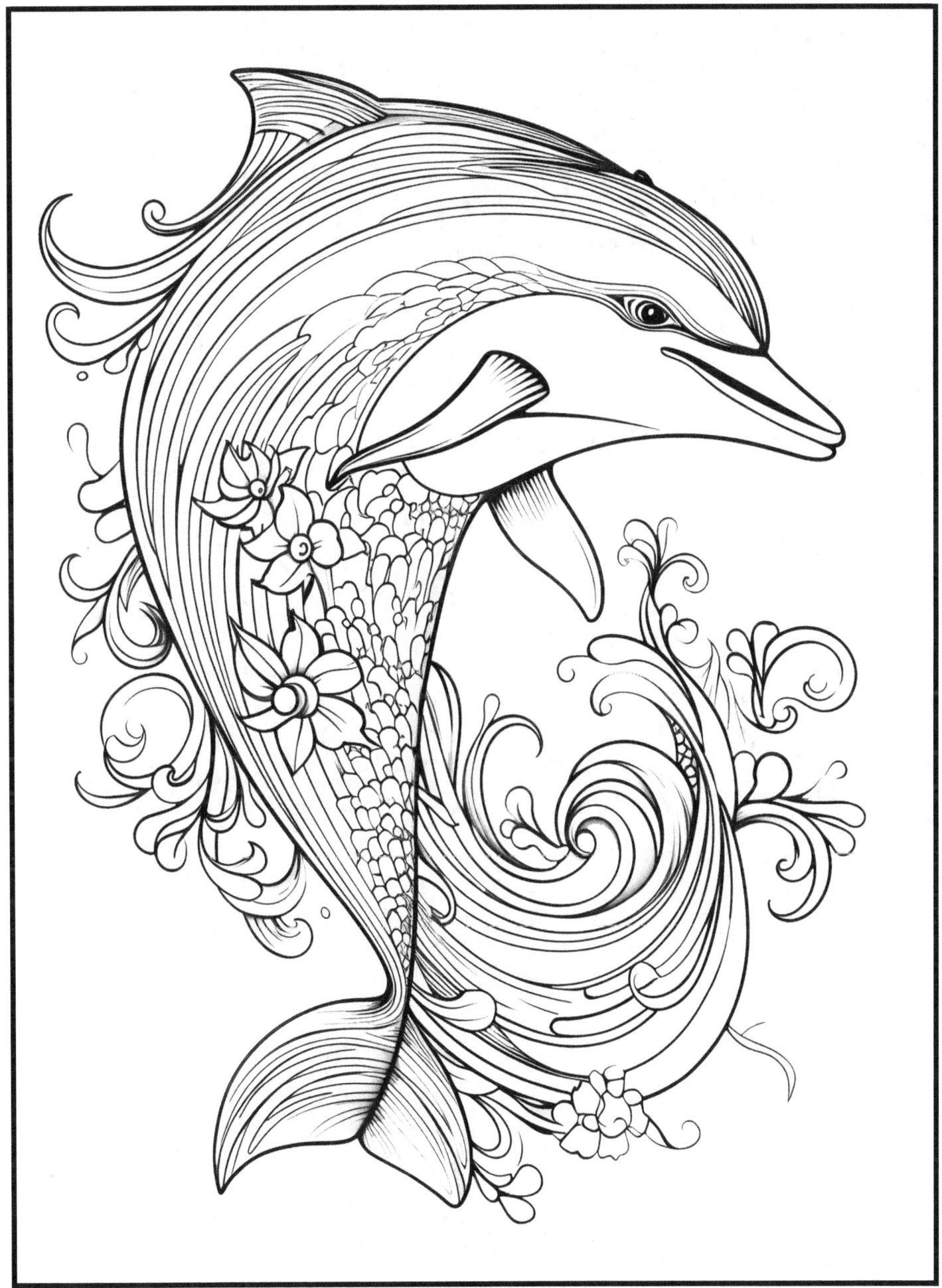

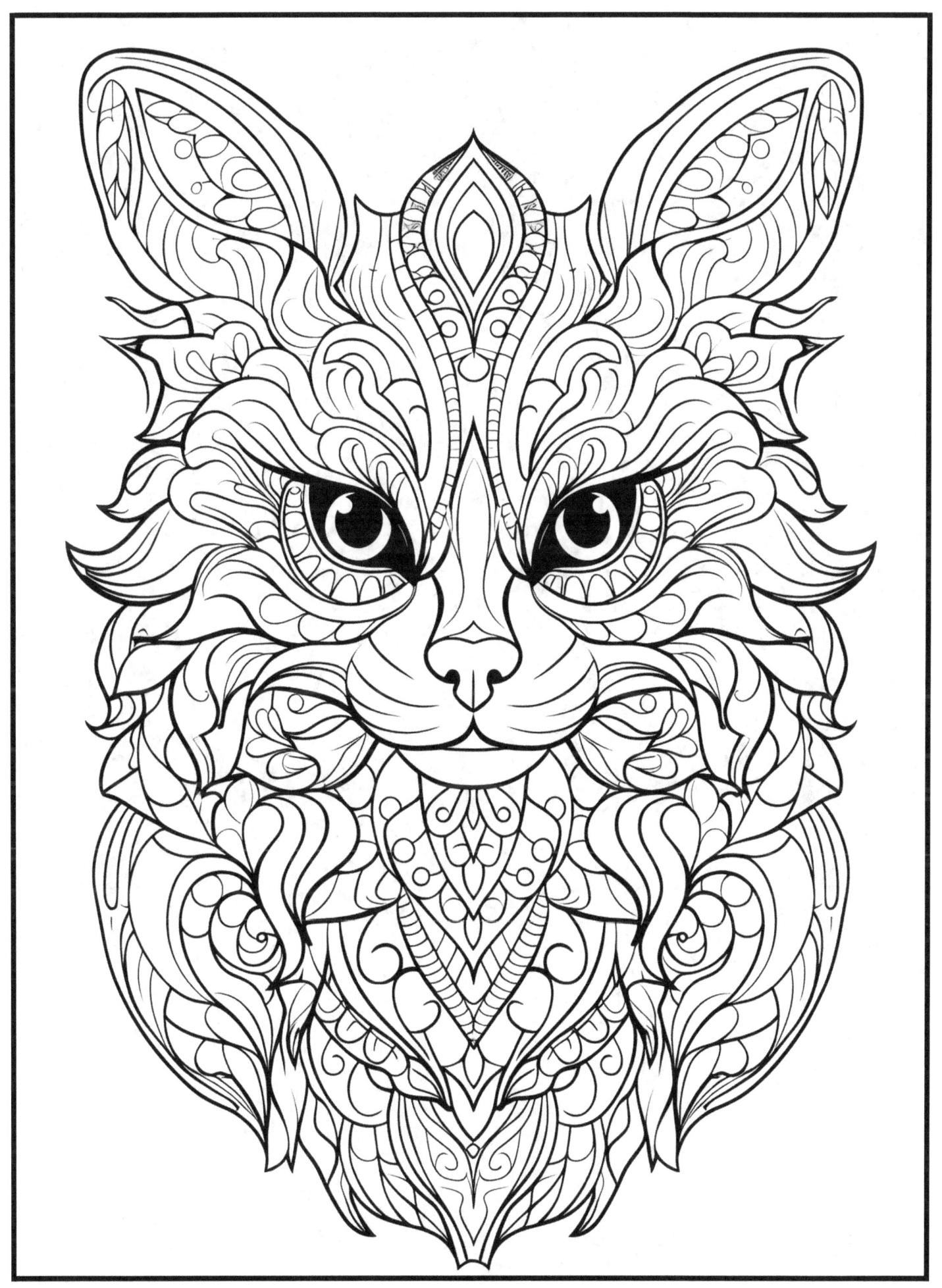

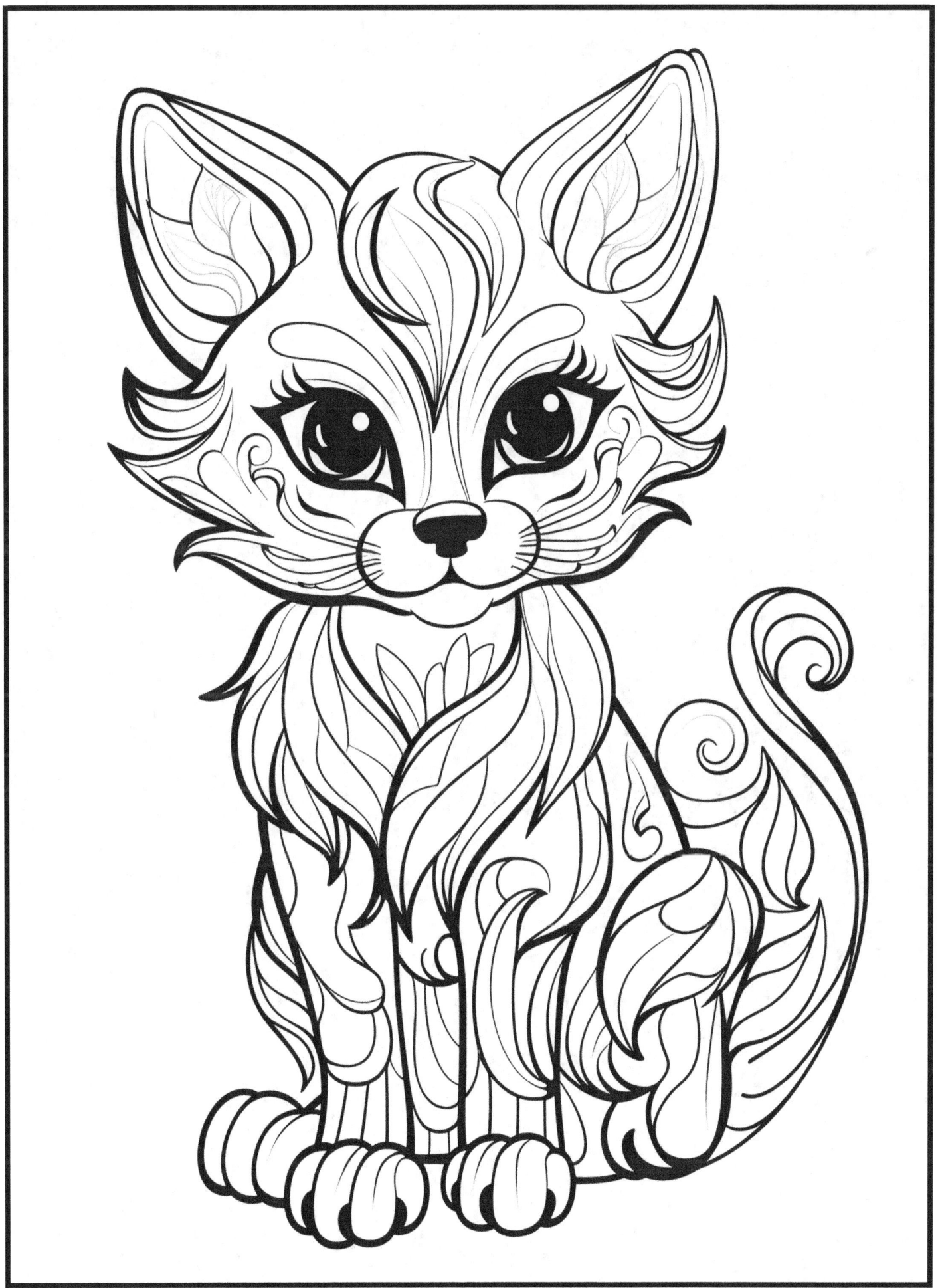

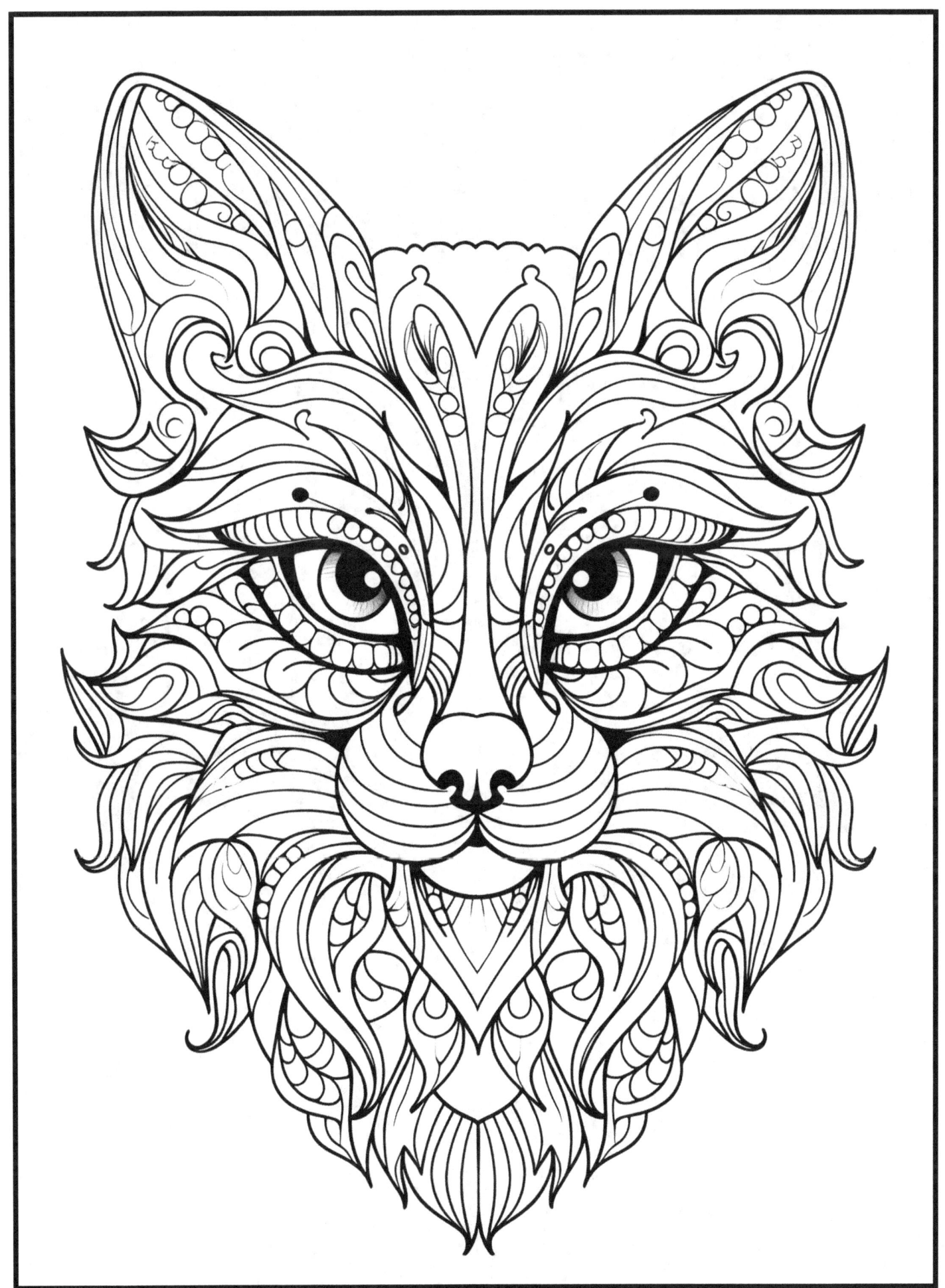

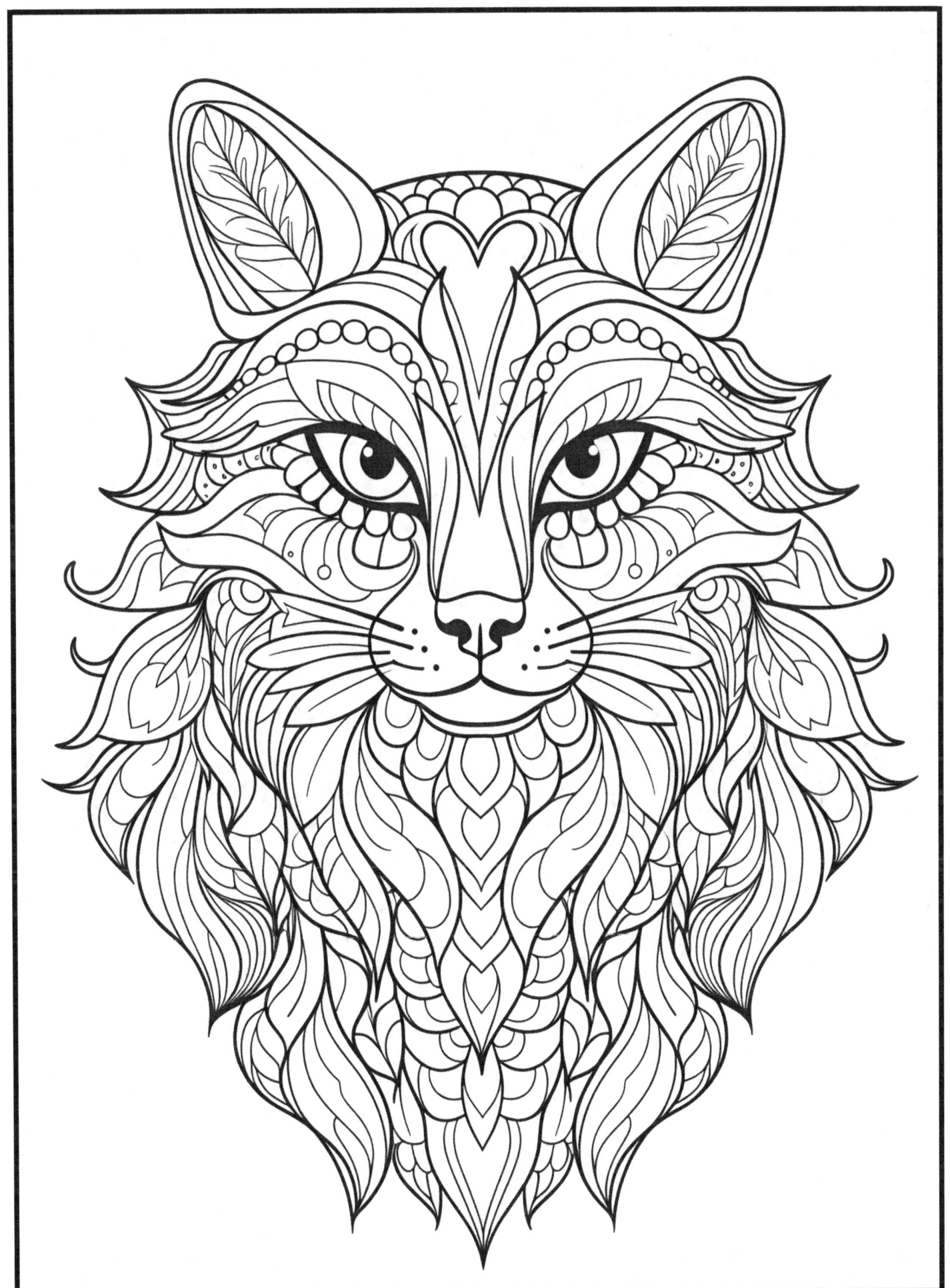

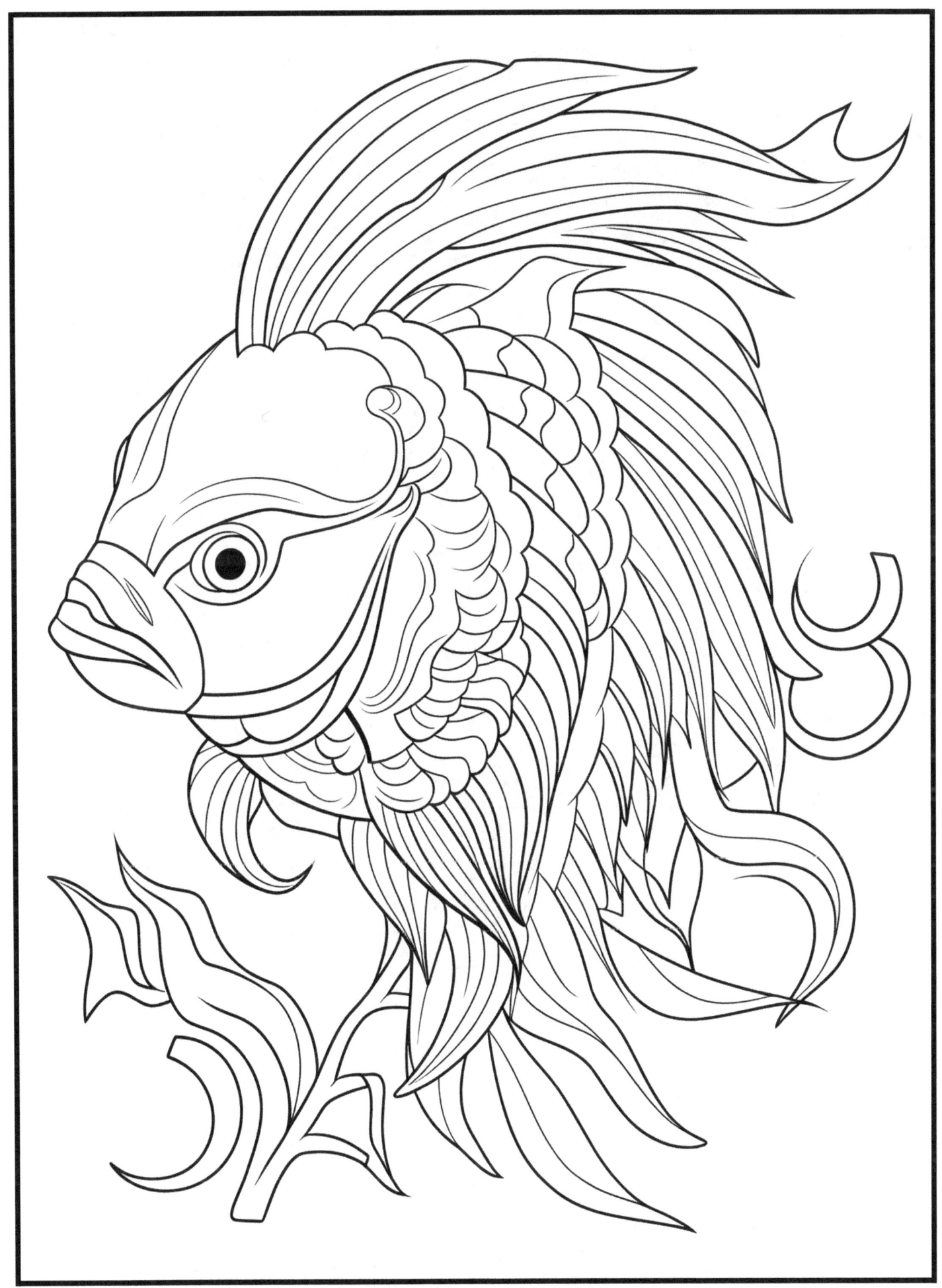

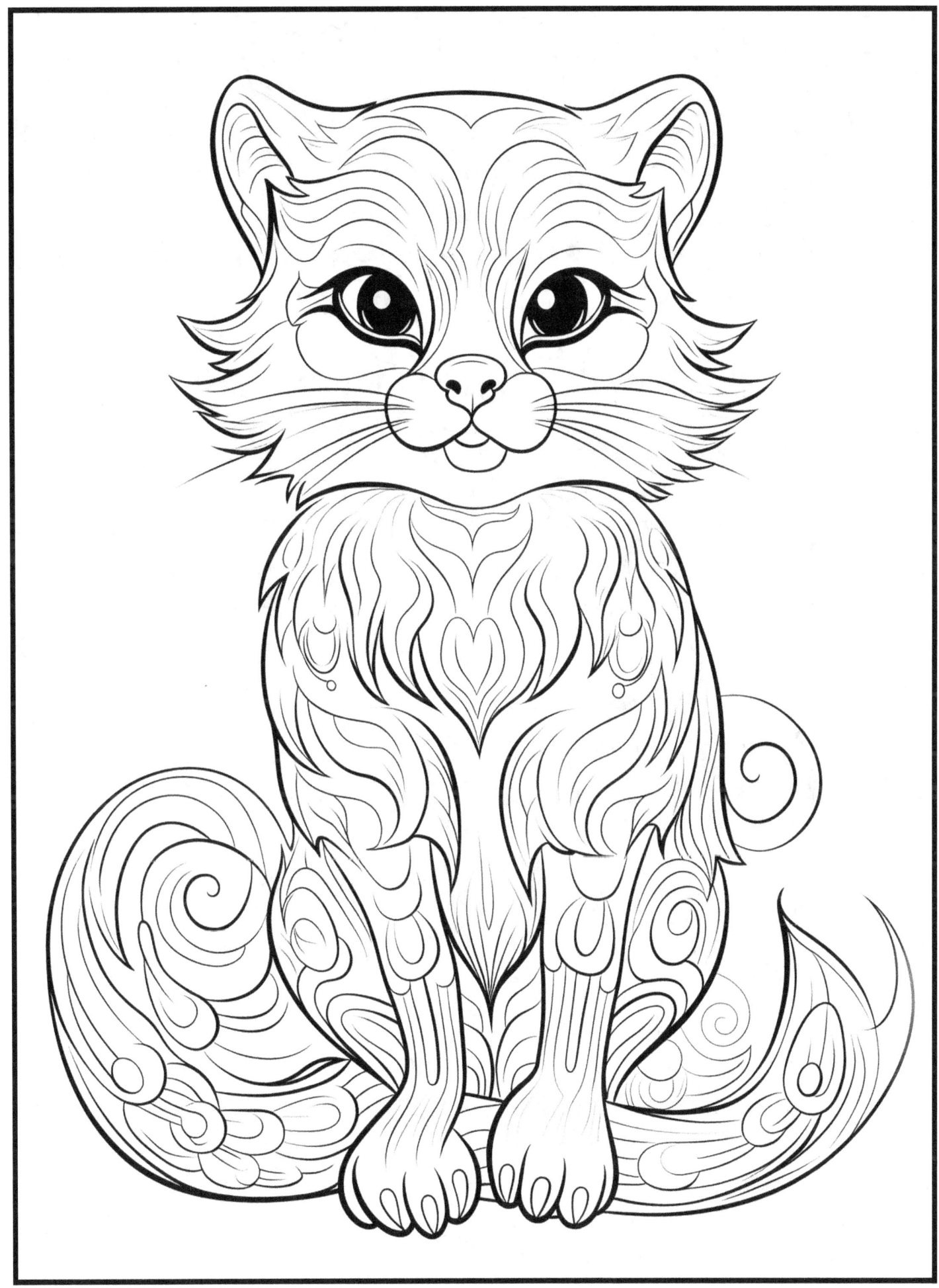

Dedicated to the animals that make our world more beautiful and astonishing.